HOOPSEEN RECRUITING GUIDE

THE TRUTH ABOUT PLAYING AT THE NEXT LEVEL

MIKE EDDY

Introduction

Basketball has been a part of my life for as long as I can remember. I fell in love with the game at eight years old and as I grew up I always dreamed of playing college basketball. As a high school player I didn't have much sense for how recruiting or exposure worked. I was the captain and one of the leading scorers and rebounders for a successful and recognized high school program. I was fairly competitive in the local AAU tournaments I played in throughout middle school and high school, but no Division I offer ever materialized. I didn't know how to evaluate myself at the time, nor did I have anyone really coaching me through the recruiting process. Looking back knowing what I do now, I probably shouldn't have been surprised that DI schools weren't calling. While I was a good high school player and better than most of the people I knew, I didn't realize that playing Division I basketball requires a fairly rare combination of hard work and god given talent.

During my Junior and Senior years of high school I started receiving some interest from a number of different Division III schools. Ultimately, out of pure love for the game, I decided to continue playing basketball in college. Playing Division III basketball isn't something you necessarily do for the glory or recognition. As with any college sport I found it was challenging to balance the demands of the sport with academics and a social life on campus. Looking back though I am really grateful for the experience and the opportunity to continue playing the game I love. I was able to be a part of a special team, a fraternity of other guys who played alongside me. I built lifelong friendships, challenged myself and made some incredible memories as a college basketball player.

Today, I continue to be involved in prep basketball and for the past 14 years have sat at an interesting intersection between college coaches and prospective student athletes. This began with my involvement as the owner and operator of a multi-court facility in Atlanta, GA called Suwanee Sports Academy (SSA). Over the past 14 years, SSA has hosted many of the best players in the country and been a connection place for thousands of eventual scholarship offers. If the courts at SSA could talk they would have some amazing stories to tell. They might

1

tell you the story about a baby-faced, 130 lb guard from Charlotte, North Carolina draining corner 3 after corner 3 in front of the coaching staff of his future college home, Davidson(who would offer him later that day) - and would go on to be a 2 time MVP of the NBA. They would tell of Hall-of-Fame coaches watching, evaluating and searching for the pieces to help them win their next championship. They might tell you about the knack for competing and winning of the likes of Jaylen Brown, Brandon Ingram, Josh Okogie and Jawun Evans. The NBA is full of players whose story includes a few stops at SSA. The courts have played witness to guys like Jonathan Isaac and Zion Williamson going from "who is that kid" to elite national prospect in the course of a weekend. Just as importantly they would tell the story of the thousands of other prospects who have gone on to play DII, DIII, NAIA and low major basketball.

In 2010, I founded HoopSeen to better serve as an intermediary between potential college prospects and the college coaching community. Instead of just serving as a host to other tournament organizers we began running tournaments and showcases to help facilitate the recruiting process for players. Through HoopSeen we started a recruiting website, hired writers and scouts, and have built a platform that is widely recognized across the country. It's been incredibly rewarding to be a part of helping kids pursue and realize their dreams.

You don't have to be around the recruiting process long to understand for every top 50 recruit, there are hundreds of really good basketball players who could benefit from having the right platform and people helping connect the dots to the next level. That's really who we want to help serve and who this book is written for.

If I am honest, this guide came together in part out of sheer frustration. In a world where information is now so readily available, it is amazing how little is understood by the average parent, coach and player about the real truths of recruiting. With poor information comes poor decisions and we see too many of the wrong decisions being made every year. I was tired of watching so many well-meaning adults trying to help a player realize his dream, but unknowingly working against the process or stressing themselves and their player out for no reason.

2

Over the years our HoopSeen staff has had a front row seat to the recruitment process of thousands of players. What seems like common sense to us often isn't obvious for the parent or player who is entering the recruiting and exposure game for the first time. That's not their fault though. There are just not many good credible resources for parents to turn to and a lot of bad information circulated through grassroots hoops. Hopefully, this guide will help set the record straight and help demystify things so parents and coaches can make more informed decisions as they help players pursue their dreams of playing college basketball.

For me it was important that this guide wasn't just one person's opinion or just the opinion of our staff at HoopSeen. This book is about how to earn an opportunity to play college basketball, so who better to help answer questions about recruiting than college coaches themselves. In preparation for writing this guide we surveyed nearly 100 Division I college coaches - we had head coaches, assistant coaches, small school coaches, high major coaches and a good sampling of most everything in between. Many of the topics in this guide have been framed around the answers given directly by college coaches. We felt like there were some important questions that the reader would benefit from a lot more if it came straight from the source, the guys who will ultimately be offering the scholarships.

Lastly, I wanted to write this guide because of the positive impact basketball has had on my life, particularly the opportunity to play beyond high school. I wanted to play Division I basketball but it wasn't something that was in the cards for me just as it won't be for a lot of the people this guide will hopefully reach. The good news is that there are far more opportunities to play college basketball outside of the NCAA Division I level then there are opportunities within it.

Despite not earning a Division I scholarship I feel lucky to have landed where I did. I received a great education, earned a degree, built strong relationships, played a lot of ball and had some fun along the way too. My hope is that the following pages will help players (and their parents coaches) evaluate where they might fit at the next level and have the information they need to maximize their chances of having the type of experience I did - at whatever level that may be.

Table of Contents

Section I - Setting the Record Straight
Recognition vs. Exposure

Exposure is one of the most overused words in grassroots basketball. It's used so often as a descriptor in basketball that it's hard to define what it even means anymore. Before we dive into the topics of this guide, we thought we should start by distinguishing between two terms: exposure and recognition. Our definition isn't necessarily the way the rest of our industry would describe them, but we think it is very helpful to understand the differences. As a parent or a player recognizing how recognition differs from exposure will help give you peace of mind as you navigate the landscape of recruiting.

Our HoopSeen team defines exposure as positive visibility to college coaches. In our opinion the goal of exposure is to earn a scholarship to a school you want to attend, and the only way to do that is to attract the attention of college coaches. This is different than recognition, which we define simply as a form of public acknowledgement of a player's ability or performance.

Recognition can take many forms. It could be winning a tournament and winning all tournament honors. It could be a mention on social media or a video clip on youtube. It could be a ranking or just informal verbal acknowledgement by some other coach, parent, scout or spectator. It may be a reputation you establish in your city or state or amongst teams you compete against. These are all positive things but they aren't necessarily the same thing as exposure the way we are defining it (positive visibility to college coaches).

The reason that most of the recognition, the tweets, the first place finishes at tournaments and the youtube highlights don't qualify as exposure is because 99% of that stuff is ignored by college coaches. If it doesn't increase your positive visibility to college coaches, it's not really exposure. Almost every day at HoopSeen we are told by parents that they are playing for a certain team, attending a certain camp or tournament because they want their kid to have more exposure. In many cases they think they are getting exposure when in reality the situation really only offers recognition. In some cases parents are misled by a well meaning but misinformed coach. In others situations the term exposure is thrown out as a hollow marketing term.

During HoopSeen events we recognize great performances all of the time, and our recognition is usually appreciated by the player as well as the coach and parents of the player being recognized. That recognition doesn't always translate to exposure though. We will publish an all tournament team for the 7th graders playing in a local tournament, and even though HoopSeen.com is one of the most read recruiting websites in the country by college coaches, those 7th graders being identified are not getting exposure - they are getting recognition.

We could take advantage of our position in the market and call everything exposure but we don't. There are certainly times and events when exposure is important and there are others where it's more about just recognizing great performances. Some people in our industry might think we are crazy for being so transparent. We could tell "Little Johnny's" parents that if he plays with us we will get him "exposure," but if he is a middle school player (and is not clearly the next Lebron James) that would be misleading if you define exposure the way we do. As we will discuss in more detail later exposure isn't really even a category for pre-high school players. There are exceptions but as a general rule college coaches don't watch middle school players nor offer them scholarships. In many cases college coaches don't have much interest in Freshmen and Sophomores either. If exposure is positive visibility to college coaches then for most players exposure doesn't really even exist until a player is a Junior in high school.

There are two primary reasons college coaches don't have much interest in players until late in high school:

1) They don't have time to wait 5 years to develop their program hoping that the now 8th grader will help them down the road. Many college coaches won't even be at the same school in 5 years. They have to win next year. A college coach recently explained to me the way he thinks many schools are prioritizing their recruiting and the progression they go through in thinking about how to fill their roster each off-season. They start with college transfers, guys who are at other schools that may be unhappy or not playing enough at their

current school but could help the program. In 2016 there were over 800 Division I transfers according to VerbalCommits.com, which equates to more than 15% of Division I boys basketball players transferring in one off-season. Next, he said many programs look for Juco players who have developed and now have the grades for a four year school. After that, they start looking at Seniors and maybe Juniors in high school. The reason they prioritize this way even though the transfer or Juco may have less eligibility is that they need guys who can come in and make an immediate impact. This is an obvious generalization, but it gives you a sense of the college coach perspective and priorities. When you need to win now, you need players who can help your team immediately. An eighth grader can't help you, but a 20 year old Juco transfer with two years of college level strength and conditioning might.

2) The second reason college coaches wait is that so much changes during the course of high school. We will chronicle this in our assessment of middle school rankings later, and how few of the top players in middle school remain at the top through high school. Because we get to see so many kids development from elementary to high school through our various tournaments we have mountains of anecdotal evidence of this as well. It's amazing how often the best players at younger ages (maybe because they grew early or had really good skills early on) end up being just average high school players or how often the clumsy kid nobody ever notices ends up exploding into the spotlight (seemingly out of nowhere) his Sophomore season of high school. College coaches know kids will change. Why waste time trying to guess how kids are going to develop when it can be so unpredictable?

Ultimately, a young player will get to the point where he is in the position for exposure. Over the years we have been fortunate to help connect the dots for hundreds of players who have gone on to earn college scholarships. A lot of college coaches have come to trust the opinions we offer because we do our best to respect the true recruiting process and our role in it - which is to pass on objective intelligence at the right time and provide a platform that makes it easier on coaches to sift through the noise.

At the end of the day, though, exposure is really up to each individual player. It's their performance on the court that will determine if they ultimately receive a scholarship offer, not what someone tweets about

7

them or ranks them. In some cases a tweet or a ranking might translate indirectly to exposure, but in many cases it won't.

Statistics of Playing at the Next Level

Now that we have spent some time differentiating between recognition and exposure, we will turn our attention to what it takes to play Division I college basketball or even go beyond to play in the NBA. It's probably already obvious to most people that it takes a pretty special mix of talent and hard work. You may already know that the odds are slim for most high school players to earn a Division I scholarship and the odds of playing beyond that are staggeringly small. In our calculations using data from the NCAA and the NFHS we put the odds of a high school player earning a Division I scholarship at around 0.8%. The odds of going on to the NBA is around 0.03% - that's a select group to say the least.

The problem with statistics like these is that it can be hard to contextualize what they really mean. We spent some time breaking these numbers down to try to give players and parents some other ways of thinking about what it will take to play Division I basketball and maybe some new ways to honestly assess where they stand.

The Odds of Playing at the Next Level

First, let's walk through how we arrived at our original odds for playing Division I basketball and the odds of making it to the NBA. There are 351 Division I schools offering men's basketball. Each school can offer up to thirteen full scholarships, which means there are 4,563 full scholarships available for Division I men's basketball (schools can also offer partial scholarships, but for our purposes we will assume only full scholarships). That seems like a lot of scholarships, but consider that there are around 540,000 boys playing high school basketball in the U.S. (NFHS:2014). Divide 4,563 scholarship by 540,000 players and you get to less than 1% of all high school basketball players will receive an athletic scholarship to a Division I school. This doesn't even account for foreign players who might also earn many of the 4,563 scholarships.

Now let's talk about going from college to the NBA. Our Editor-in-Chief at HoopSeen, Justin Young, always says to make it to the NBA you have to win the DNA lottery. Consider the following: Every year sixty players are drafted by NBA teams. On average, twelve of those players are foreign, leaving forty-eight slots for U.S. players. To simplify the statistics, let's assume boys playing high school basketball are split evenly across grades and so are Division I scholarships and NBA draft picks.

Now picture yourself as one of 135,000 seniors who are playing high school basketball in the U.S. Only 1,100 of the 135,000 of you are going to have an opportunity to play Division I basketball on a scholarship. As we said, less than 1% of all high school players.

ODDS OF PLAYING AT THE NEXT LEVEL

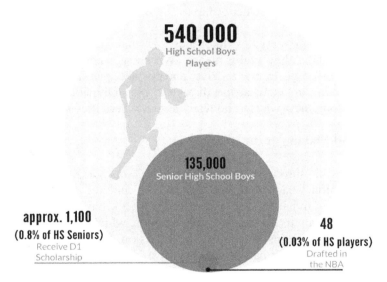

540,000
High School Boys
Players

135,000
Senior High School Boys

approx. 1,100
(0.8% of HS Seniors)
Receive D1
Scholarship

48
(0.03% of HS players)
Drafted in
the NBA

Sources: NFHS-2014 & CDC

60 players drafted but on average 12 are foreign born.

Only forty-eight of the 135,000 players will one day be drafted by an NBA team, about a 0.035% chance (1 in 3,000). Even if you are drafted that still doesn't guarantee you will ever earn a spot on an NBA roster.

Now that you know how we arrived at our odds of playing at the next level let's walk through some different ways of making this more concrete. In the chart on the next page we approximated the number of Division I scholarships available to high school seniors and asked what would happen if those scholarships were distributed proportionately based on a state's population? Obviously, basketball is not played evenly around the country so the actual numbers will vary. Some states will have more scholarship players and some will have less than indicated in the chart. Nevertheless, take a look at your state and the number of scholarships available to seniors based on a state population distribution. It's certainly not perfect but it might give you a good general idea of how competitive you have to be to make it to the Division I game if you simply look at about how many scholarships are available per capita and consider your state only.

What we hope you will see is that in most cases being the best player on your high school team is not nearly good enough to become a Division I player. In many cases being the best player in your region or district won't qualify you either. When you consider all of the teams and players competing in high school basketball around your state, you can see from this chart there really aren't many scholarships to go around. You could take this analysis further yourself and divide the number of scholarships for your state by the number of classifications offered by your state high school athletic association to see how many scholarships are offered by classification. For example, if your state (based on population) has thirty scholarships and six classifications of play, then within each classification you might have on average Division I scholarships to go around each year. If you live in a state like this, are you one of the five best players in the entire state in your classification?

Again this analysis doesn't account for the fact that basketball is also an international game, and there are plenty of foreign-born players who are also vying for some of those scholarships. If you account for them, the odds of playing Division I are even more difficult.

Not all prospects are created equal.

You have probably noticed that basketball is a vertical game and taller players have a natural advantage. If you are blessed with great height, the statistics we have discussed so far actually move in your advantage. If you aren't tall, the statistics of making it to the next level are even more challenging.

A seventeen-year-old boy, 6'4" or above, falls in the 99.43% of height (Source: CDC). To be conservative with our analysis, let's assume every high school boy 6'4" or over in the U.S. plays high school basketball. Since there are about 8.6 million high school aged boys in the U.S. (Source: U.S. Census 2012), that would translate into 49,000 high school basketball players in the country who are 6'4" or above assuming every boy over 6'4" played basketball. If you divide 49,000 by the total number of boys playing high school basketball in the US then at most 9% of all high school basketball players will be above 6'4".

Now that we know, conservatively speaking, that over 90% of high school basketball players are under 6'4" we can look at the breakdown of actual Division I college basketball rosters to see what percentage of Division I basketball players are also under 6'4."

We sampled sixty-six Division I college rosters and found that approximately 44% of college basketball players are 6'5" or below.* Why did we not use 6'4"? Because we recognize some players might continue to grow after seventeen years of age and that roster heights are not always accurate. Again, our analysis isn't perfect but our goal is only to provide further context to consider.

Based on our conservative assumptions, we can conclude that about 90% of high school players (those 6'4" or below) vie for 44% of Division I scholarships. Those that are 6'4" or above, which is less than 10% of high school players vie for the other 56% of scholarships. Height is a huge indicator of the odds of making it to the Division I level.

If you are 6'4" or above, your odds go from less than one in 100 to better than one in 20 chance of earning a Division I scholarship. If you are not at least 6'5", your odds go from one in 100 to less than one in 200. In other words, players who are 6'5" and above are probably at least ten times more likely to receive a Division I scholarship than players who are not.**

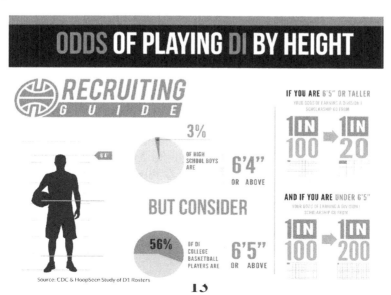

*We randomly sampled two team rosters from every Division I conference and found that out of 927 players, 521 were listed over 6'5."

**Our analysis does not factor in foreign players receiving Division I scholarships, which would make the odds even less likely.

Don't Forget the non-Power conferences

There are thirty-two Division I men's basketball conferences. How many can you name? When most people think about Division I sports, they naturally gravitate toward schools from the five Power Conferences (ACC, Big 10, SEC, Pac-12 & Big 12). But schools from the Power Conferences only hold about 18.5% of the available scholarships for Division I men's basketball.

Remember that Division I basketball is a lot bigger than just the select teams who you see playing on television or in the NCAA tournament. Even if you are good enough to make Division I, which few players are, the likelihood of earning an offer from a power conference school is even far more selective. Only about 0.15% of High School players will earn a scholarship to a power conference school.

Again to try to contextualize this a bit more, let's return to a state-level analysis. HoopSeen provides national and state rankings of every high school class. Our home base is the state of Georgia, and we have published rankings for the top thirty-five players in the last three graduating classes in Georgia. All of the players who make this list each year are special talents. These guys were all-state players, hometown heroes, state champions, and almost always the best player whenever they stepped on the court.

We have 451 high schools under our main state athletic organizing body. Even if you are number thirty-five in our state rankings of players, it's very, very difficult to make this list. Now consider that out of the last three graduating classes in Georgia, only eight players who weren't ranked in the top ten in their class have gone on to a Power Conference school. Many of the best players in a state loaded with talent end up in conferences like the Atlantic Sun, Colonial, Big South, Conference USA, and dozens of other conferences.

If you are a player reading this, we hope it motivates you to work hard. Playing Division I basketball takes talent and a lot of hard work.

Hopefully, these statistics will help you realize how hard you really do need to work.

If you are a parent or coach reading this, we hope it helps you to set the right expectations you have for your athletes. Hopefully, it helps you better understand what is ahead and opens you up to considering other incredible opportunities in the sport. As we mentioned, most of the Division I opportunities fall outside of the teams you see on TV. There are also some amazing opportunities for your athlete within Division II, III, and NAIA basketball. We'll talk about those later.

The Real Timeline of Recruitment

If you have never gone through the recruiting process, nothing can be more stressful or create more uncertainty than not knowing when certain things should begin to happen. When do most players begin to get recruited? When do I need to start worrying about exposure? When will colleges begin offering players scholarships?

Our HoopSeen staff has had a front row seat to the recruiting process of thousands of high school players. We talk to college coaches every day about players they are recruiting, and many colleges subscribe to information our staff provides about recruitable prospects. In addition, every year thousands of college coaches sit on the baselines and stands at our tournaments watching for kids to whom they might want to offer a scholarship. A lot of people will offer advice on exposure and the process of getting exposure, but in many cases parents and players are being completely misled on the timing of how it actually works.

As a general rule, if you are not in high school, college coaches are not interested. Exposure before high school doesn't really exist. In our survey of almost 100 D1 college coaches, we asked if they ever watched or recruited players in eighth grade or below. 100% of them responded that they did not watch or recruit pre-high school players. If "exposure" is about getting positive interest from the guys with the scholarships, then according to the coaches we surveyed you won't find it.

We also asked college coaches, of the scholarships they have offered in the past two years, what percent were offered to players in eighth grade or below? 100% of the coaches we surveyed said they had made zero offers to players in eighth grade or below.

We'll talk about high school players next, but before we move on, here is a point we want to highlight. If you are not in high school don't make your decision on what teams to play on or what tournaments to attend based on exposure to college coaches. Anyone who is in eighth grade or below who tells you that playing with them will get your child exposure is either misinformed or misleading you.

16

At HoopSeen we recognize younger players all of the time during and after tournaments, and we have one of the most read recruiting websites in the country. But that recognition does not necessarily translate to exposure as we have defined in this book.

For the majority of players, recruiting and exposure does not begin until a player's junior or senior year of high school. Many parents and travel coaches we talked to are stressed when the recruitment of their freshman or sophomore player isn't taking shape, but they really shouldn't be. Again, don't take our word for it, here is what college coaches had to say; 95% of the college coaches we surveyed said they spent less than 10% of their time recruiting and watching freshmen. About 50% of the coaches we surveyed said they spent less than 10% of their time recruiting and watching sophomores. No coach said they spent more than about 25% of their time watching and recruiting sophomores. On average, the coaches we surveyed said they spent about 75% of their recruiting time on juniors and seniors.

This point is even clearer when you look at scholarship offers. On average, only about 9% of college coaches' offers go to freshmen or sophomores. Over 90% of offers go to juniors or seniors.

Here is my anecdotal story that really drove the thought home that college coaches didn't have much interest in players until their junior year of high school. Several years ago HoopSeen was hosting the annual Bob Gibbons Tournament of Champions during the Spring NCAA evaluation period. This is one of two weekends Division I college coaches can go out and watch recruitable prospects at a travel team tournament. It was championship Sunday of the Gibbons and all morning the facility was full of college coaches. As the day went on, teams were eliminated until we were down to the championship games in three age groups. On one court we had the championship for 17U - rising seniors. Next to that court was the 16U championship game consisting of rising juniors, and finally next to the the second court was the 15U championship, which consisted of rising sophomores.

I walked past the 17U court and it was packed, standing room only, with college coaches shoulder to shoulder around the court. Next to it the 16U court had a smattering of college coaches. It wasn't empty but there were noticeably fewer coaches watching the 16U championship than the 17U game. I walked down to the final court where the 15U teams were playing and there was not a single college coach watching the game. What is interesting is that the 15U court was, in our opinion (at HoopSeen), the one with the most long-term "talent" by far of the three championships we had going on that day. Those kids who played on that court are in college now and there were about 15 Division I prospects playing on that court, including several players who are now playing major college basketball and an eventual McDonalds All-American. At the time I couldn't believe it. There were players in the 15U game who would have been stars in the 17U game on the first court. We knew there was a lot of talent, but the college coaches just weren't interested and these kids were about to be sophomores in high school.

As a grassroots basketball culture, we are painting the wrong picture. On the next page compare our chart of what many people think the recruiting timeline looks like with what it looks like for most players.

There are always exceptions, and it's the exceptions that create the angst and misunderstanding for those who aren't getting exposure. Some of the really talented players (the top 1%) may see this timeline creep up and on some very rare occasions a college will offer an eighth grader. But those are by far the exceptions and not the rule. This isn't based on theory for us either. We have seen the same thing play out for hundreds of players every single year.

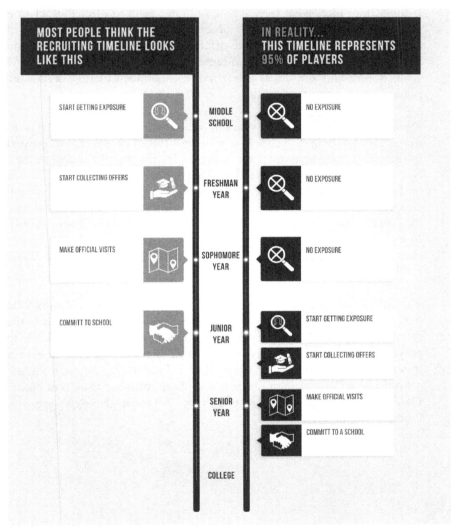

Here is generally what most players can expect, assuming they do have the talent to play at the next level. During a player's junior high school season, he might have some colleges start expressing interest in recruiting him. Schools may attend the player's high school games or practice. If there is mutual interest, the school may elect to recruit him during the spring and watch the player play travel ball during the NCAA evaluation periods in July.

If the school likes what they see, they might elect to offer the player a scholarship in the spring of his junior year of high school. Many will also elect to wait to make an offer until after the July evaluation periods. During the summer colleges will continue to watch the now rising senior and additional offers may be extended in July before the player's senior season begins.

During the fall of a player's senior year it's common for a player to make official visits to schools who have offered or are still interested in recruiting the player after the summer. Some players will sign their National Letter of Intent right before the beginning of their senior basketball season (November). For many players the recruitment will continue to play out even during their senior basketball season and they may sign a National Letter of Intent in the early spring (April). Some players may go all the way to the end of their senior year before their recruitment and future plans for the following year become finalized.

This is a simplified version of what takes place for many players who play college basketball. There are many different ways the recruitment process can play out, and it varies greatly from player to player. Our purpose is to give you an idea of what is normal to expect in terms of the timeline of a player's recruitment. If you are a middle school player, a freshman or even a sophomore, your time will come. Don't get too worked up if you haven't gotten the exposure you thought should have by now.

How College Coaches Find Prospects

We have defined exposure as positive visibility to college coaches. This visibility occurs directly when a coach watches a prospective athlete play, train or practice through one of the following formats:

- College coaches can watch players during their high school season by either attending a game or practice.
- College coaches can watch players during travel tournaments taking place during the spring and summer evaluation periods. Non-Division I coaches have more flexibility to watch throughout the season.
- College coaches can watch players who come to campus for a camp.
- College coaches can watch game film or highlight videos of a player.

How coaches determine who they want to go watch and potentially recruit is usually influenced by more indirect visibility.

Scouting services: The NCAA certifies and approves certain scouting services that NCAA coaches can subscribe to each year. Generally speaking a college program will pay a fee to the particular scouting service or services they want to utilize for access to evaluations, intelligence and contact information on prospects. Scouting services can be a meaningful path to exposure - indirectly. Influential scouting services may help raise a player's profile. In many cases college coaches will utilize scouting services to help them build out their plan for who they want to go watch during recruiting periods as well as during the spring and summer evaluation periods. A good review from a scouting service can go a long way.

However, college coaches do not award scholarships based on scouting services alone. At some point they will want to see a player play with their own eyes and probably want to see the player play on multiple occasions before they offer a scholarship. A scouting service may help by making a prospect a priority for coaches to go watch, but players will ultimately have to earn the scholarship based on a college coach's own evaluation too.

Also, keep in mind that the subscriber base and influence of various scouting services varies greatly. Some scouting services have only one or two college programs as subscribers and others have hundreds of programs who take their service. Some services don't even offer thorough and regular reports or updates to college coaches about prospective athletes. Which begs the question why would a college program subscribe to a scouting service that doesn't really produce valuable information on prospective athletes? They might still subscribe because of the perceived influence a particular person who owns the scouting service has with certain players or groups the program wants to recruit. In recent years the NCAA has added regulations on the scouting service industry and established more rigorous standards for selling services to college coaches to try to prevent college programs from paying for influence. The bottom line is just because someone says they have a scouting service doesn't always mean that they can or will help a player with exposure. This is where it's important to do your homework, talk to your high school coach, travel coach or others in the know about whether a scouting service is credible or not with college coaches.

High School Coaches: High School coaches can be a good resource for indirect exposure and players should get their high school coach involved in their recruitment early on. Many high school coaches have had other players who have been recruited at some point and they may have a good understanding of the recruiting process as well as the level you are capable of playing in college. Many high school may have also developed a network of college coach contacts through the recruitment of their former players or they may have developed a network of friends and former colleagues who coach or have influence at the college level. Even if your high school coach doesn't know the coaching staff at a particular college a phone call from a high school coach to a college can go a long way in helping gain some attention from a college program.

Informal Networks: Many of the best recruiters in college basketball are incessant networkers. They know who the influencers are in different areas and many have built a trusted network of people who can help them identify talent. These networks may consist of a variety of sources - travel coaches, high school coaches or friends who stay abreast of the current recruiting landscape.

Exposure Camps or Tournaments: Exposure camps and tournaments that do not take place during the April or July evaluation periods will not have any Division I coaches present. Some of these exposure camps and tournaments may have DII, DIII, NAIA and Juco coaches in attendance though. If the Exposure Camp or Tournament is outside the evaluation period then it will only provide Indirect Exposure to Division I coaches to the degree of the influence that the scouting service running the camp or scouting services attending the camp have with college coaches.

Exposure camps and tournaments outside the evaluation period can be beneficial, but make sure to do your research first. Do the organizations running or attending the event have a real platform to college coaches? Will they take the time to watch, evaluate and report what they see? If the answer is yes to these questions and you play well then an "exposure event" can be really helpful.

Also, remember college coaches are not interested in scouting reports or rankings on middle school kids so any camp or tournament that touts itself as giving exposure to middle school players is not providing exposure in the way we are defining it. That's not a knock on those camps. They can still be very beneficial from a development standpoint or as an opportunity to compete against other good players. Players may also receive some recognition from those running the camp, but they most likely will not translate into positive visibility to college coaches.

Choosing the Right Travel Team

"I want to make sure my kid gets exposure. How do I choose the right travel team?" We hear this question from parents all of the time. We get it too; this is stressful stuff. Parents want to get this right and put their child in the best position to succeed. What is one to do when faced with a variety of teams to choose from and no clear criteria for deciding which team will deliver successful exposure? Unfortunately, we see situations all of the time where a kid plays with one program for multiple years, develops great relationships with teammates and a rapport with the coach, only to leave because a parent is concerned that the old team isn't garnering his or her child enough exposure.

Before we answer this question, though, let's quickly revisit our definition of exposure we laid out at the very beginning of the book. Exposure is positive visibility to college coaches, and that is very different than what most people are calling exposure today. Exposure does not equal rankings, mixtapes, social media mentions, or "exposure camp" participation. There is nothing wrong with any of those mediums, but they don't all translate to exposure unless they are positively increasing the visibility of a player to the guys with the scholarships.

Now that we are hopefully on the same page on how we are trying to define the goal of exposure, let's try to answer the question on how to choose the right team. If your child is in 10th grade or below, this answer is pretty simple. Choose the team that maximizes the opportunity for your child to develop their skills, competitiveness, and confidence. If you are seeking to increase the probability for positive visibility to college coaches, then focus on helping your child become the best player and teammate he can become first. As we just discussed in the previous section, college coaches are spending very little time watching teams below tenth grade.

If you get a "sales pitch" from a travel coach who tells you your child should play on his team because he will get him the most exposure, and that coach is not coaching a tenth or eleventh grade team, then you should be highly skeptical. They are either misleading you or confusing what exposure really is. As we outlined in the previous section no matter how good your child is in the sport, if they are not at least a sophomore, it is not likely for a college coach to spend the little time they have watching your player. And we know until they do, they aren't offering them a scholarship either. Every single coach we interviewed said they would not offer a player a scholarship without seeing that player play first.

The point we are trying to make is that your child will have an opportunity for visibility to college coaches. But unless he is a 6'9" rim destroyer in eighth grade, his first real opportunity for exposure probably won't occur until his junior, or often, his senior year of high school. For 95% of kids who do get recruited, their recruitment usually does not take shape until their junior year or later. If your child is younger than a junior and you are worried about "exposure," then you can take a deep breathe for now. The only players getting ahead are the ones who are getting better at the game itself.

If your kid is not a junior in high school, just focus on getting him ready for his time. Think about what kind of coaching, experiences, and skill sets will prepare him for his window of exposure to college coaches. Here are a few of the considerations we recommend for parents thinking about this question:

1. Try to find a travel team that will emphasize individual skill development. If your child gets a year or several years of focused skill development, that is going to be a competitive advantage when he is a junior in high school competing for a scholarship. Most kids overplay and under-develop in the offseason. Try to find a program that will give you some balance. Competing on a team is helpful and motivating, but don't lose sight of the time working on individual skills and weaknesses.

2. It doesn't matter if you are on a really good team if you never get any playing time. Find a team where your child will get to play important minutes. They don't necessarily have to start, but if they don't ever play they won't develop confidence and competitiveness in a game environment.

3. Keep in mind that the person coaching your child will have a tremendous influence on him as a person. What values do you

want your child to pick up? Look for teams who have coaches who reflect those values.

4. Find a program that balances the number of games and amount of travel for what your child actually needs. You don't have to spend every weekend of your spring and summer at a different tournament. Too many teams (especially younger teams) are overplaying and under-developing. We also see a lot of teams who travel out of state when there are plenty of competitive options near them. It's fun for the kids and families to travel some, but most teams don't need to travel very far to get the competition and development they need. If you are playing on a team that travels to other states all of the time, you may want to ask why? If you aren't regularly winning competitive tournaments in your city, then you don't need to travel to find better competition. And as we have already illustrated, we also know, if you aren't in at least tenth grade, you aren't traveling for exposure either. Traveling to tournaments in other areas can be a great experience for a team, but it can have diminishing returns if you travel all of the time.

5. If you have younger players, be wary of teams who limit your child to one position and area of development. We see this all of the time; a kid matures before most in his grade and because he is bigger has to play and practice as a post player with his back to the basket. Over time everyone else catches up in size, but he never had an opportunity to develop other skill sets he now needs to compete.

6. Find a team where your child is going to grow more confident each year as a player. This happens through the coach and how his coaching style and philosophy mesh with your kid's personality. If your child wants to play at the next level, help prepare him so when he is a junior he has been challenged before, played in difficult environments, and has built a confidence for how to compete.

How to choose a program when your child is a junior in high school

For the most part all of the considerations mentioned above should continue to be important factors for choosing a team even when a player reaches the window for exposure. For example, it doesn't help a player get "exposure" if they are on the most competitive team but most of the time they just sit on the bench.

The coach or key person in the program who will be helping you and your player navigate the recruiting landscape is important. Their experience and track record of helping other kids play at the next level is certainly something that should be considered, and they should be able to clearly articulate to you how the team will help your child with exposure for playing at the next level.

As you talk to coaches, try to find someone who will be honest with you instead of telling you what they think you want to hear. It sounds great when a coach tells you your child could start in the ACC as a freshman, but if he is really more of a low D-I player it would be so much more helpful in the long run to have the right expectations. It's not that you can't continue to dream, but by the time your player is a junior in high school, a coach who will set some realistic expectations for your player's recruitment is more important. You want to find a coach who will promote your child, but if that coach is not realistic at what level he is promoting he may turn off schools who would recruit your child because it will appear that you don't have reasonable expectations.

Knowledge and experience with the recruiting process is important, but it's also important that the person helping your player with the process really cares. Don't discount coaches who have maybe a little less experience but who you know and trust. You can't overvalue a coach who really cares about your kid and who you know is going to work hard to put your kid in a position to succeed.

Don't get lost in the brands. When it comes to travel basketball, college coaches don't care about the name on the front of the jersey. They don't really even care which travel team wins or loses a game. They are looking for talent. Certainly some travel teams are more recognized than others, but scholarships are not handed out based on the reputation of your travel team. Find the most suitable team for your player. If he is good, the coaches will find him even if he isn't on a team with a big reputation.

Finally, do a little research yourself on the recruiting process. Simply by being informed you will be in a better position to navigate the question of which team you should play for. And remember, if your child isn't a junior in high school yet there is no reason to be stressed out about exposure.   He will have his time, but right now it's all about becoming the best player he can be.

What's with These Sneaker Teams?

Nike, Adidas, and Under Armour all sponsor travel basketball programs around the country. The numbers vary from year to year, but in general each sneaker company has historically sponsored between twenty-eight and forty programs in any given year. While there are changes each year there is generally very little turnover in teams. Nike and Adidas have sponsored teams for decades, and quite a few of each company's original teams are still under contract.

What makes these teams sponsored is that they sign multi-year contracts with one of the three sneaker companies. The teams usually get some annual commitment of a combination of shoes, gear, uniforms, and cash. The team program director can usually allocate those resources as he sees fit. One of the commitments the teams make as part of their agreement with the sneaker company is to participate in sneaker-sponsored events during the spring and summer. Nike, Adidas, and Under Armour will each run a "circuit" of four to five tournaments or league stops between April and July. The teams who participate in those events are the officially sponsored teams. Sometimes there will be secondary divisions or add-on tournaments around the sneaker company event, but the teams playing in the secondary division aren't really "sponsored" teams.

Why do sneaker companies sponsor high school travel teams? What is their ultimate goal? It seems that they have two primary objectives. The first is to build brand loyalty at a young age with potential future pro basketball players. The theory is that if they can get a player wearing their gear and playing in their circuits and camps, then when that player turns pro he will sign with them instead of their competitor. The second objective, which is related to the first, seems to be to try to build loyalty so that the player might choose a college that is also sponsored by the same sneaker company as the player's travel team. Nike, Adidas, and Under Armour all have significant interests in the success of many of the college basketball programs they sponsor and would love the top prospects to choose a college that is aligned with the shoe company's interests. Why the NCAA is complicit in this arrangement we aren't quite sure, but that is a discussion that falls outside of the scope of this guide.

Back to the point, the shoe circuits are primarily targeted toward the 17U (juniors/rising seniors) and secondarily to the 16U (sophomores/rising juniors). Younger teams that are part of these same programs are not necessarily "sponsored" or "officially" participating in the shoe company circuits. Sometimes we hear eighth grade parents say things like, "My child will be playing in the EYBL" (Nike's circuit), but they don't realize the EYBL is really only offered for 17U. Some of the 16U teams will participate in the same tournaments, but the EYBL, Adidas Gauntlet, and Under Armour Association isn't even offered to eighth graders.

If you are concerned whether your child is playing on one of these circuits, we understand the attraction, but until they are 17U you shouldn't worry too much about it because there is no such thing as a sneaker-sponsored circuit or sneaker-sponsored team until later in high school.

There are thousands of travel teams wearing uniforms from Nike, Adidas, and Under Armour who are not a "Nike Team," "Adidas Team," or "Under Armour team." Some will claim that they are because they wear a certain uniform and shoes. They might even get an attractive team discount from a team supplier of uniforms. If you want to know who is actually one of these shoe company teams just visit the EYBL website, the Adidas Gauntlet website, or the Under Armour Association website.

If you are a travel coach holding out hope you will one day get a "sneaker contract" for your team, you should know that new teams are added on very rare occasions. If you have a really good player or players, the sneaker companies would much prefer one of their existing programs try to recruit your players to their team rather than offer a new program a contract. If you think you can beat the odds, look up the sneaker-sponsored teams in your state. How long have the existing programs been sponsored? When was the last time there was a change to that lineup?

In recent years there has been an overemphasis from parents and travel coaches over the importance of the shoe company circuit for exposure. That's not a diminishment of those circuits (they are excellent for exposure); it's just that there are plenty of exposure opportunities for college bound players outside the context of the shoe circuit. If you are not on the shoe circuit, you can still get plenty of exposure and find plenty of scholarship offers.

For some players it's even a benefit to not play in a sneaker circuit because they get to play on a team where they are one of the featured players instead of on a team where they might come off the bench and play limited minutes. College coaches don't make offers because a player sat on the bench on a really good travel team. They make offers because they watch a player perform on the court. The most important thing for a player is to play for a coach and in a system that will allow him to highlight his strengths. If that happens to be on a sneaker-sponsored team, that's great. If it happens to be on a non-sneaker-sponsored team, the college coaches will still find the players who can help their program. If you are not currently a top 100 ranked national prospect, in some cases it actually might be easier for coaches to find you on a really good team without a shoe affiliation.

Are Rankings Important?

Player rankings are discussed a lot in grassroots basketball circles. There are numerous media and scouting groups in basketball who publish rankings of some sort or another. "What's he ranked?" is a question we hear all of the time from the casual fan who is trying to judge the quality of a player. Most of the groups creating rankings are interested in attracting eyeballs to their websites, and nothing drives traffic like new rankings. Without a doubt the highest viewed pages on HoopSeen.com are the rankings pages. When we update our rankings we see a dramatic spike in web traffic.

The question is how important are rankings in the "exposure" equation? They likely do have some influence on college coaches as a player gets closer to graduation, but most coaches understand the limitations that rankings have on actually predicting how a kid will ultimately perform in college. Rankings can be fun to talk about and debate. It's also nice as a player to be recognized in someone's rankings, but rankings are incredibly subjective and have some pretty significant limitations. Here are just a few of them in our opinion:

1.   What are we ranking? Are we ranking a player's potential, what scouts call a player's ceiling, or a player's current skill, size and athletic ability. Ask anyone who ranks players and everyone will give you a slightly different answer. Some want a finished product now and rank accordingly. Others like the idea of what the player could be as his game and body mature and rank accordingly.

2.   Hidden Agendas. Often rankings are influenced by other factors than the player's actual ability. As the saying goes; "You scratch my back and I will scratch yours" (travel coach, parent, etc . . .) It's probably not uncommon for a player to get ranked a little higher than he should because the "ranker" has some conflict of interests or pressure from others.

3.   Natural Biases. First impressions are important in basketball rankings too. A player might play thirty games in a travel

season and play great all year but the scout ranking him happens to see him during a poor performance. There are plenty of others biases as well. For example, some scouts have a preference for bigger guards, and others don't care as much. Some scouts are highly impressed by shot blocking, and others are not. Rankings are part beauty contest. What may impress one person doesn't quite do it for the next.

4.   How do you watch the entire country? National rankings are inherently difficult because it's just not possible to watch every player enough times to know exactly whether the fifth best point guard in California is one notch better than the fifth best point guard in North Carolina. Even if you could watch them each 100 times, the decision on who is better might just come down to preference for style of play.

5.   GroupThink. Part of the reason many scouting services will arrive at very similar rankings is that most people don't want to take the risk of having a contrarian thought. Group think sets in as people read each other's rankings until there is ultimately very little difference in one rankings from the next. That is why every year there are at least a handful of players who go on to college unranked who end up becoming standouts, and there are always a handful of highly ranked players who don't pan out.

While rankings can make for interesting discussion, they are, at best, approximations of a player's ability, and college coaches understand this. The biggest and most important limitation of rankings is time. It's hard to predict how a player will develop, and as you move farther away from a player's graduation from high school, the rankings become even less predictive.

At HoopSeen we don't rank players before the conclusion of their sophomore year of high school. Part of this is philosophical, but part of it is that rankings players any younger is highly misleading for what will actually play out and sometimes creates unfair expectations and pressure. Even the rankings of sophomores will change dramatically before graduation, and we have our fair share of misses.

In our survey of college coaches we found out that virtually no college coach watches or recruits players in middle school. We suspect that they don't pay too much attention to middle school player rankings either. All of the problems we have outlined for why ranking any player is difficult are magnified at the middle school level. In the table on the next page we have a list of the American-raised players in the class of 2015 who were selected in the first two rounds of the NBA draft. Next to their name we have how they were ranked as eighth graders by a "National Middle School Rankings" group. Only one of the eleven guys selected in the NBA draft was ranked as an eighth grader. The one player who was ranked was 6'10' as an eighth grader.

	2016 DRAFT PICK	8TH GRADE RANK
BRANDON INGRAM #20 SF | 6'9" 190 lbs | Los Angeles Lakers College:	2	PLAYER NOT RANKED
JAYLEN BROWN #7 SF | 6'7" 225 lbs | Boston Celtics College:	3	PLAYER NOT RANKED
JAMAL MURRAY #27 SG | 6'4" 207 lbs | Denver Nuggets College:	7	PLAYER NOT RANKED
MARQUEESE CHRISS #0 PF | 6'10" 233 lbs | Phoenix Suns College:	8	PLAYER NOT RANKED
HENRY ELLENSON #8 PF | 6'11" 245 lbs | Detroit Pistons College:	18	PLAYER NOT RANKED
MALIK BEASLEY #25 SG | 6'5" 196 lbs | Denver Nuggets College:	19	PLAYER NOT RANKED
MALICHI RICHARDSON #5 SG | 6'6" 205 lbs | Sacramento Kings College:	22	PLAYER NOT RANKED
DEJOUNTE MURRAY #5 PG | 6'5" 170 lbs | San Antonio Spurs College:	29	PLAYER NOT RANKED
DEYONTA DAVIS #23 PG | 6'10" 240 lbs | Memphis Grizzlies College:	31	PLAYER NOT RANKED
DIAMOND STONE #0 C | 6'11" 255 lbs | Los Angeles Clippers College:	40	PLAYER NOT RANKED
STEPHEN ZIMMERMAN #35 C | 7'0" 240 lbs | Orlando Magic College:	41	13

Believe it or not, if kids are old enough to dribble a ball someone will be ranking players. We found some national middle school rankings for when the 2017 graduating class were sixth graders. The list is included below. Next to each name is the player's final ranking as a high school senior:

CLASS OF 2017 RANKINGS 6TH GRADE TO SENIOR YEAR

CLASS OF 2017 RANKINGS: FROM 6TH GRADE

	PLAYER	HOMETOWN	POS.	HT.	SR. RANK
1	JAYLIN **FLEMING**	Chicago, IL	PG	5'2"	Not Ranked
2	PAUL **WASHINGTON**	Frisco, TX	C	5'8"	28
3	DAMON **HARGE**	Mountain House, CA	CG	5'0"	Not Ranked
4	CHRIS **GILES**	Allen, TX	C	5'9"	Not Ranked
5	NATE **PIERRE-LOUIS**	Plainfield, NJ	F	5'4"	Not Ranked
6	CALEB **NERO**	Tulsa, OK	G	5'2"	Not Ranked
7	JESSE **NELOMS**	Memphis, TN	PG	5'1"	Not Ranked
8	NOJELL **EASTERN**	Chicago, IL	F/G	5'6"	47
9	MARQUES **WATSON**	Brooklyn, NY	PG	5'1"	Not Ranked
10	MICHAEL **PORTER**	Fort Wayne, IN	F	5'9"	3
11	CHASE **HAYDEN**	Memphis, TN	G	5'2"	Not Ranked
12	CEDRICK **LATTIMORE**	Detroit, MI	C	5'9"	Not Ranked
13	KYLE **SMALL**	Anaheim, CA	PG	4'10"	Not Ranked
14	SCOOTER **SMITH**	Norwalk, CA	G	5'4"	Not Ranked
15	MILES **JOHNSON**	Lakewood, CA	C	5'10"	Not Ranked
16	SELASSIE **BOURNE**	Brooklyn, NY	PG	4'9"	Not Ranked
17	JAMAL **NIXON**	Plainfield, IL	F	5'9"	Not Ranked
18	TYSHON **ALEXANDER**	Charlotte, NC	F	5'8"	99
19	REGINALD **CRAWFORD**	St. Louis, MO	C	5'9"	Not Ranked
20	DAVID **VASQUEZ**	West Linn, OR	G	5'2"	Not Ranked

The point is not to knock "rankings" (they can be fun) but to keep rankings in perspective as a predictor of the future. They are intended more for fans than college coaches. A high ranking as a middle school player doesn't necessarily translate into a good high school player. In fact, it can even be a detriment if a player thinks because he is rated high that he doesn't have to work as hard.

It may be nice to receive the recognition, but 100% of the college coaches we surveyed said they would never offer a player without seeing him play first. In high school a player might have an opportunity to finally play in front of college coaches, but what a player was ranked as an eighth grader will be completely irrelevant to their decision to make an offer or not.

Section II: NCAA Concerns

What you need to know about NCAA Academic Requirements

Every year we see too many players who have the talent to earn a Division I or Division II scholarship but don't meet the NCAA academic requirements to qualify for eligibility. In a HoopSeen survey of college coaches we asked if academic eligibility concerns factored into whether they recruited a player or not. 40% of coaches said they would likely not recruit a player who could be a major contributor to their program but who they perceived might not qualify academically. Another 49% of coaches said it would influence their decision; so over 90% of coaches said that academics would be a factor on whether they even recruited a player.

College coaches have limited time and limited scholarships to offer. The last thing they want to do is spend months recruiting a player, watching him play, and holding a scholarship spot for him to find out that he can't play for the program because he doesn't meet the NCAA's academic standards.

The standards have become more difficult in recent years and can also be a little difficult to understand. We will attempt to outline the criteria below, but would highly suggest visiting with a school counselor early on in high school. Don't wait and get behind on your academics. The clock starts in ninth grade!

Three Areas of Academic Qualification
In order to meet the academic eligibility requirements you have to meet three standards:
1. GPA - Minimum of 2.3 in core courses
2. Completion of 16 Core Course Hours
3. SAT or ACT score - Scales based on GPA

If you fail to meet any one of these three standards when you graduate high school, you will not be eligible for Division I basketball.

Start Early
The GPA requirement and core course requirements mean you can't wait until your junior or senior year of high school to get serious about academics. What you do as a sophomore and even freshman year can impact your academic eligibility.
GPA

This is the easiest of the criteria to understand. You need a minimum of a 2.3 GPA. The only caveat is that the GPA is calculated based on your core courses only. If you have a GPA that is higher than 2.3 that can take some pressure off your performance on the SAT and ACT. The higher your GPA, the lower required score on the standardized tests. Just remember you can't "pad" your GPA with non-core courses like PE. Those courses will not affect the GPA calculated to determine NCAA eligibility.

Core Courses
You can determine which courses at your high school qualify as core courses by visiting the NCAA website.

You need sixteen credits to qualify, but one class does not equal one credit. Most high schools break their calendar year into either two semesters or three trimesters. Most classes in semester-based schools count as .5 credit. Most classes in trimester-based schools count as .34 credit.

In other words, if you are at a school on the semester system you might need thirty-two classes (not sixteen classes) to reach sixteen class credit hours and forty-eight classes in a trimester school to reach sixteen class credit hours. In most cases you will probably need to average four core courses per semester/trimester for all four years of high school in order to qualify academically.

Core vs. Non-Core
Generally speaking, standard math, English, natural and physical science, and social science courses are considered "core courses." Other academic courses may also qualify such as a foreign language and religion.

There are many high school courses that are not considered core. Most fine arts courses (i.e. music, dance), physical education courses, and vocational courses (i.e. driver's ed) are not considered core courses and will not count to the sixteen course credits you need to qualify.

Also, remember not all "academic" classes such as math, English, and science necessarily qualify as core. Qualifying math classes must be Algebra 1 or above. Remedial classes or classes taught below grade level are generally excluded from being considered core courses.

Also, remember that you need a cumulative GPA of 2.3 or higher in core courses. An A+ in physical education will not help raise your GPA from the NCAA criteria because it's not a core course. Also, if you retake a class you cannot count that class as a core course.

Test Scores
The test scores required vary based on your GPA in the core courses. The scale can be found on the NCAA website.

If you have the minimum GPA of 2.3 you will need a combined score of 900 for the SAT or 75 for the ACT. By comparison, a 3.5 GPA would require the student athlete to only score 420 for the SAT (combined) or 39 for the ACT (combined).

You do not have to take both the SAT and ACT. Either score can qualify you. Also, you can take either test as many times as you want. The NCAA will accept your best score.

A couple other tidbits
- The requirements outlined above are for participating at the NCAA DI level. NCAA DII, NCAA DIII, NAIA, and Juco all have different academic requirements. In general, the NCAA DI has the most stringent academic guidelines.
- The NCAA will allow an athlete to take a "Redshirt" year if they don't meet the 2.3 GPA minimum but have a GPA better than 2.0
- The NCAA will allow some limited post-high school work to help an athlete reach the core requirement hours.

40

Official and Unofficial Visits

Before an athlete commits to a school, he will certainly want to visit some of the schools he wants to consider attending. The good news is that there is no limitation on the number of unofficial visits a player takes, and there are no restrictions on the time of year those visits are taken.

Unofficial Visits

During an unofficial visit the player and his family may meet with the coaching staff (as long as they aren't visiting during a "Dead Period"). The only expense that the school may cover during an unofficial visit is they can provide three complimentary tickets to a home sports event. The athlete and his family is responsible for any other expenses (lodging, food, etc . . .) during an unofficial visit.

Official Visits

A player may begin making official visits after January 1 of his junior year, but there are some important requirements that have to be met first. The player must provide the school with proper test scores from the SAT or ACT as well as a copy of his high school transcript before the official visit. In addition, the player must have a certification account through the NCAA eligibility center.

If all of these things are in place, a player can begin making official visits as early as spring of his junior year. Since most players' recruitment is still taking shape during their junior year, most official visits are completed during a player's senior year. For Division I and Division II schools, players are limited to no more than five official visits and can make no more than one official visit per school. At the Division III and NAIA levels a player can take more than five official visits but still no more than one per school. A player may make as many unofficial visits as they want to a school in addition to the one official visit.

The purpose of the official visit is for a player and his family to get to a college campus and get a feel for what it would be like to attend school and play basketball there. The player will usually meet with the coaching staff, meet current team members, attend a class, tour campus, watch a practice, and often attend a home football or basketball game. There might be several or more prospective players visiting the school at the same time.

An official visit can last up to forty-eight hours. The school can pay for the travel, lodging, food, and "reasonable" entertainment expenses of the player and his family while on the official visit.

Official visits can be an important signal

Keep in mind that Division I basketball schools can only offer twelve official visits per year. That's not a lot of visits when you consider those visits could be split between seniors and juniors. If you are invited on an official visit by a school, that could be a strong indication of how interested they are in you. On the other hand, if a school is recruiting you but hasn't offered you or seems to be reluctant to invite you for an official visit, that may indicate they are still recruiting someone in front of you.

While you cannot invite yourself on an official visit, you can certainly ask about it to gauge how serious a school really is about recruiting you. You might ask the coach if he intends to invite you on an official visit. How they respond to that question at different points of the recruiting cycle might give you an important signal. If you ask in February of your junior year and they respond with, "we'll see in the fall," that may not mean much. They want to see you play in the spring and summer first. If it's your senior year and the school has been recruiting you for a while, and they balk at the idea of an official visit, that might tell you a little bit more about their level of interest.

While being invited on an unofficial visit is a good sign and one you should take advantage of as much as possible, remember, schools can offer unlimited unofficial visits. If a coach does invite you on a visit he will generally clarify which type it is, but if you aren't clear it can never hurt to ask.

Beyond Division I College Basketball

As we have discussed already playing Division I basketball is incredibly competitive. There are thousands of high school basketball players each year vying for a limited number of roster spots on a Division I basketball team. Fortunately, there are other options for players who want to continue their playing career beyond high school.

National Collegiate Athletic Association (NCAA)
The NCAA has three levels of competition. The different levels are generally indicative of a school's size, athletic budget, and number of athletic scholarships available. The NCAA divisions help create parity, and national championships are offered at each division. According to the NCAA, only about 3.4% of high school players will continue on to play at one of the three NCAA levels.

Division 1: consists of about 350 schools with the largest budgets and most scholarships to offer. Almost all of the college teams you see on television are from Division I schools.

Division 2: consists of about 300 schools. Division II schools have scholarships to offer, but fewer than Division I schools. Often Division II schools will offer partial scholarships. These schools are generally smaller and have smaller athletic budgets than Division I schools.

Division 3: this is actually the largest NCAA division by participation. There are around 450 schools that fall into this category. The biggest difference between Division 3 and Division 2 is that Division 3 schools do not offer athletic scholarships. Many Division 3 schools do offer academic or need-based aid to student athletes.

National Association of Intercollegiate Athletics (NAIA)
The NAIA is a college athletic association with about 300 member institutions. The NAIA consists mostly of small and medium sized schools and has two divisions of play. NAIA schools may offer athletic scholarships, but like many NCAA Division 2 schools, partial

scholarships are common. Compared to the NCAA the rules for recruiting and participation are less stringent for NAIA schools.

National Junior College Athletic Association (NJCAA)
The NJCAA supervises a national association of accredited junior colleges and two-year institutions. In basketball circles, playing NJCAA is usually referred to informally as Juco, short for Junior College. Like the NCAA the NJCAA has three divisions of play. Division I schools can offer athletic scholarships. Division II schools can also offer scholarships but have some restrictions, and Division III schools cannot offer athletic scholarships. By definition a junior college is only a two-year program, but it can be a good option for some athletes who want to eventually play at an NCAA or NAIA school.

In particular, Junior Colleges can be a good option for players who may not meet the academic standards of NCAA programs. A year or two of junior college gives a player an opportunity to continue to play and develop while also becoming academically eligible to transfer to a NCAA school later. For some players Junior College might make sense if they don't have scholarship offers to play NCAA basketball but want to keep playing as well as developing their skills for a possible scholarship offer later. For the non-scholarship player, junior and community colleges are generally less expensive than four-year

schools. Keep in mind that the NCAA limits a player to four years of college basketball eligibility and Junior Colleges count against that eligibility.

Post-Graduate Programs

In recent years there has been tremendous growth of post-graduate basketball programs around the country. A post-grad program offers a player a year between graduating high school and starting his college basketball career. As opposed to attending a community or Junior College for a year, the player does not lose one of his years of eligibility to play at the NCAA level.

For most post-graduate programs, the idea is that certain players would benefit from another year of development, training, and higher level of competition before committing to a college program. In many cases the player may not have any scholarship offers or isn't satisfied with the level of the offers he does have, and opts to wait another year to see if his recruiting will continue to take shape as he plays for a post-grad team and gets more exposure from playing an extra year.

While post-grad schools can be beneficial for some players, there are certainly no guarantees a college scholarship offer will come at the conclusion of it. Some post-grad programs can cost close to the same as a year of college tuition, so the decision to take a year in between high school and college should obviously be considered carefully. Many post-grad players will finish their year without a scholarship offer and still have to pay for four years of college tuition to earn a college degree. A post-grad year can certainly help players, especially, players who need more time to develop their skills or grow into their body, but if a player really isn't good enough to receive a scholarship offer, post-grad is not necessarily going to change that reality either.

Everyone wants to say they play "D1"

The wonderful thing about sports is that they can open doors to new opportunities and experiences a person might not have otherwise. That's why we encourage players who are really passionate about the sport to think beyond DI. Look at the statistics. There are just not many high school basketball players who are going to make it to the Division I level.

On the other hand there is some really high-level basketball being played every year in NCAA Division II, NCAA Division III, NAIA, and Junior College. Too many young players assume that anything below Division I is below them. But if a player doesn't have any Division I offers, then they should rethink what level is appropriate for them. Remember, only 3.4% of all high school basketball players play in the NCAA across all levels.

We encourage players who want to play college basketball, but are not being recruited by Division I schools, to go watch a local Division II, NAIA, or Junior College game. Better yet, tune in for the Final Four of the NCAA Division II or Division III basketball championships, which are usually aired on television. You might be surprised at the quality of the better programs in some of these leagues other than NCAA Division I.

The question on how you should conduct your recruiting comes down to your objective. What are your priorities? Is it important that you go to a program where you will have a chance to play and contribute meaningfully? Is the academic reputation of the school important? Is the scholarship and/or financial aid to help with the tuition of college important? Are your career opportunities after basketball important? OR is it most important that you be able to tell your friends that you are going Division I?

If you are a good basketball player, your skills and talent can help you open doors and allow you to continue to play the game you love, even if that isn't at the Division I level. If you love to play the game, would you rather walk on to a Division I program where you will likely never play or go to a Division II school where you will have a chance to start? Some of the best academic institutions in the world compete at the NCAA Division III level. If your future beyond basketball is important, you might want to consider how you can use basketball to help open doors at a prestigious academic school. A Division I school may not offer you a scholarship or financial aid, but there might be a Division II school that will offer a partial scholarship that will save you a great deal of money and student debt.

People have different motives for playing basketball beyond high school. Some athletes get so focused on playing Division I basketball that they lose sight of the other opportunities that may be afforded to them. When you are thirty nobody is really going to care much

46

whether you played Division I or Division II or NAIA basketball, and likely neither are you. What you are going to care about is the experience and doors that were opened by playing college basketball. So stay open-minded and go watch a competitive non-Division I level basketball game. It might change your perspective.

What does Mid-Major really mean?

In recruiting terminology you will often hear coaches and scouts talk about high-major, mid-major, and low-major as they describe the different levels of college basketball. These terms actually refer only to Division I NCAA basketball. DII, DIII, NAIA, and Juco are generally referred to as such, while DI schools are informally categorized along these subjective terms.

In recruiting parlance you might hear the terms used in the following sentences: "John Doe has high-major talent," or "mid-majors should be watching John Doe," or "I think John Doe could be a low-major prospect." The problem is that the terms high-major, mid-major, and low-major have no concrete definition. They are just ways of trying to express the level of schools a player could play for.

The high-major term is the easiest to grasp in the sense that schools from the Power 5 conferences are usually what one has in mind when describing the high-major. Those conferences include the ACC, SEC, Big10, Pac12, and Big12. These are generally the teams who play on TV regularly and have large recruiting and athletic budgets. There are some schools in other conferences outside of the Power 5 that may also be considered high-majors as well. Teams like Villanova and Georgetown in the Big East and UConn and Memphis in the American Athletic Conference come to mind as good examples.

On the other hand you have a program like Gonzaga, who is probably responsible for the emergence of this terminology. They were one of the first poster children of the mid-major program emerging each spring during the NCAA tournament. For this reason alone a lot of people probably still think of Gonzaga as a mid-major; announcers called them that for years as they upset high-majors in the NCAA tournament. However, one might make a strong argument that today the Zag's reputation, history, and talent makes them a high-major school. What is one to do when the program historically most associated with a term no longer neatly fits the category?

This isn't really an important argument or something a prospect needs to spend any time worrying about. It just illustrates the difficulty in defining the different levels of Division I college basketball. We can think of a number of schools outside of the Power 5 conferences who are regularly attracting more talent and performing at a higher level than some Power 5 schools.

When you get down to the difference between mid-major and low-major, it's even more difficult to distinguish between the two levels. Conferences help some. For example, most of the teams in Conference USA, A10, and the Mountain West would fall under the category of mid-major. Some of the teams in the Big East and American would generally be classified as mid-major and some high-major. Outside of that you could have teams from just about any other Division I conference rise up to the mid-major category - especially if the program busts brackets in late March.

Our advice to prospects is to not get lost in this arbitrary and ever-changing terminology. Don't try to choose schools you may want to attend because a school has a certain label or not. There are so many other important factors to consider regarding how well you will fit in a program. Generally the level will play itself out during the recruiting process. If you don't have a high-major school recruiting you but you do have half a dozen low-major schools who have offered, that is probably a more objective feedback on what level is appropriate than any other subjective evaluation.

Also, remember most Division I players will not play high-major basketball (only about seventy-five or so schools out of 351 are generally considered high-major programs). If you consider that each program has about three scholarships per year and some of those will go to foreign players, Jucos, and transfers. It is probably safe to calculate there are only about 150 to 200 or so spots on high-major rosters for each high school class. That's a pretty select group!

The Recruiting Calendar

Recruiting for Division I basketball programs is regulated by the NCAA, and they set a specific calendar each school year specifying which recruiting activities are permissible at various times of the year. Before we discuss the actual calendar, let's begin by defining the four types of recruiting periods. For college coaches every day of the year falls into one of four categories:

1. Recruiting Periods - During the "Recruiting Period" college coaches may go to regularly scheduled scholastic (high school) basketball games, practices, and scrimmages to watch and evaluate players they want to recruit. College coaches may not attend non-scholastic (i.e. travel basketball tournaments) games or practices during this time. Other activities that are permitted during the recruiting period include official and unofficial visits, emails, phone calls, and in-person visits.

2. Evaluation Periods - The NCAA currently specifies certain times in April and July each year when Division I college coaches may attend non-scholastic-certified tournaments to evaluate players who they might want to recruit.* Both boys and girls currently have two weekend evaluation periods in April. The boys also have three (5)-day evaluation periods in July. Girls currently have two (7)-day evaluation periods in July. These evaluation periods are the time when many of the big travel tournaments are hosted. Division I coaches cannot go to any tournament they want during the evaluation periods. It must be a tournament that has been certified by the NCAA. In summary, DI college boys coaches currently have a total of twenty-one evaluation days to attend travel tournament in April and July. Girls currently have twenty evaluation days to attend travel tournaments in April, July, and September.*
*Girls have also historically had one evaluation weekend in the fall as well.

3. Dead Periods - During this period coaches are not allowed to meet with players on or off campus and are not allowed to evaluate players

in person at either scholastic or non-scholastic competition. Coaches can still call and email during dead periods.

4. Quiet Periods - A quiet period is similar to the dead period with the exception that during the quiet period coaches may meet with a player on campus during an official or unofficial visit to campus by the player.

It may be helpful to note that NCAA Division II coaches have a different recruiting calendar and Division III and NAIA coaches have a lot more flexibility to attend travel tournaments throughout the spring and summer regardless of whether the tournament is sanctioned by the NCAA or falls in the Division I evaluation period.

September through March
The recruiting calendar is fairly detailed, but it broadly follows the high school and travel basketball season. The "Recruiting Period" runs from early September through the end of March. There are a few quiet and dead days during these months, but this is the primary time when coaches can get on the road to watch players work out and play with their high school teams and for recruits to visit campus for official and unofficial visits. Basically, the recruiting period for coaches runs concurrently with the high school basketball season including the time in the fall many teams are doing pre-season conditioning and pre-season workouts. This is the time on the recruiting calendar when there is the most opportunity for personal interaction between coaches and recruits.

April
The April recruiting calendar is a little hard to keep up with, but it's mostly a quiet or dead period with two important exceptions. Currently, the NCAA allows college coaches to attend non-scholastic basketball tournaments on two set weekends in April. This is the time most high school travel teams will participate in NCAA-certified showcase tournaments as every program in the country sends out their entire staff to watch players.

May and June
May and June dates are either quiet or dead periods.

July

July offers another important time for college coaches to evaluate players. Men's coaches have three (3) five-day periods in July when they can attend non-scholastic tournaments. Women's coaches have two (2) seven-day periods in July for evaluation. Again, these are important evaluation times for college coaching staffs, and almost every Division I coach in the country will be out attending events during the July evaluation periods.

August
After the crazy July evaluation periods, August is usually a quiet period.

Of course, once school starts and high school teams begin pre-season conditioning, college coaches can hit the road once again and the cycle continues.

Section III - Navigating the Recruitment Process

Evaluating the Prospect Beyond the Court

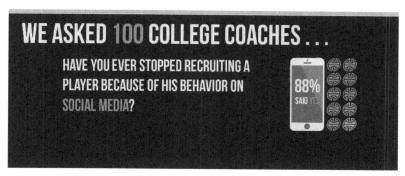

College coaches are looking for players who can help their team win. Of course, they want players who can score, shoot, defend, pass, and handle the ball, but college coaches also recognize that in order for them to win they have to sometimes look past just the skills and abilities to intangible assets and the general character of the player. From a college coach's perspective there might be a dozen or more players at a given position whom they are considering recruiting. Oftentimes the decision to start, or sometimes stop, recruiting a player very often has to do with factors other than talent.

When a college program decides they may want to recruit you, they will begin taking a deeper look at your academics, character, and key influencers in your life. In our section about academics we talked about how for many schools the question of a player's future academic eligibility is certainly a factor in recruiting decisions. Some schools will not recruit a player that they think may have trouble meeting the NCAA academic standards.

If you maintain social media accounts, you can count on the coaches recruiting you following you on those accounts. In our survey of college coaches, 100% of them said they follow the kids they recruit on social media, and 88% of them said they have in the past stopped recruiting a player because of what he was posting on social media. Think about that for a minute. If you want to be recruited to play college basketball you need to either close your social media accounts or think very carefully about the things that show up on your feeds.

What is appropriate to post on social media? It's hard to define specifically, but here is something to consider before you post:

Envision yourself at your next high school basketball game. It's a Friday night and there is a big crowd watching. Now picture yourself at halftime walking out to center court with a microphone and reading your last ten tweets out loud to the crowd or showing a video of your last five clips on SnapChat.

Before you post, consider how you would feel if what you are about to post showed up at your next high school game's halftime show. College coaches might or might not be at your next high school game, but they are definitely following your accounts.

Parents have a role in the players' recruitment as well, and every year many parents derail their kids' recruitment. 90% of college coaches we surveyed said that they have stopped recruiting a player because they thought one of the player's parents might be a distraction to the player. For many players showing up on campus and beginning college basketball is a big transition. Plus, college programs want to build a specific culture and bond amongst their teams. The last thing a

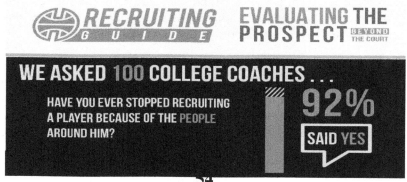

RECRUITING GUIDE   EVALUATING THE PROSPECT BEYOND THE COURT

WE ASKED 100 COLLEGE COACHES . . .

HAVE YOU EVER STOPPED RECRUITING A PLAYER BECAUSE OF THE PEOPLE AROUND HIM?

92%

SAID YES

college coach wants is an overinvolved parent distracting the player from that transition.

It's not just the parents that can derail the recruitment. 92% of college coaches said they stopped recruiting a player because of the people around him. College coaches want to recruit ball players who are focused and won't create drama on or off the court for the coach. If there is a lot of drama around the player in high school or people who have undue influence that aren't really helping the player mature and develop, then that can be a big warning signal for a college coach. Are the people around you creating unnecessary drama? Are the people closest to you the type of people who would fit with the culture and expectations of the programs you want to recruit you? Everyone is influenced to some degree or another by the people who they are surrounded by. College coaches know this and they are definitely paying close attention to who you have around you.

Intangibles of a Player

When HoopSeen hosts showcase tournaments that college coaches attend, we compile a list of the rosters of every team playing in the tournament and bind those rosters into a book we give to the college coaches to assist them in their evaluation. In some of our camps we will take an old roster book from a previous tournament and pass it around for the campers to see. There are so many teams that some of the books are two inches thick with rosters.

We ask the players to look through the book and notice the thousands of names in the book, and inform them that in each NCAA evaluation period a coaching staff make pick up a dozen or more of these type of books at other tournaments as well. It's overwhelming when you see the massive quantity of teams and names of potential future college players that a coach has to sift through and watch in just a couple days.

The question we pose to players is how do you become a player who stands out in this enormous crowd? The first part of the answer is that you have to work incredibly hard to become the best player you can possibly be. The second part of the answer is that you have to figure out a way to differentiate yourself beyond just your tangible skill sets. If you are a 6'2" guard how do you make yourself different than the other hundred 6'2" guards playing in the same tournament?

In our survey of college coaches we asked what "intangible" characteristics they looked for in players. Interestingly, all of their answers fell into one of three main themes.

1. Competitiveness. Many college coaches cited some form of competitiveness as the number-one intangible for what they are looking for in players. Some of the phrases used to describe competitiveness were "will to win," "passion," "compete consistently," and "winners on and off the court." College coaches are paid to win basketball games. The only way to building a winning culture is to have coaches and players who love to compete and step up when the game is on the line.

2. Work Ethic. Many college coaches said they are very interested in a player's work ethic. They want players who have great attitudes when it comes to working hard. Some coaches describe this as a player with a "motor." This is a term used often in basketball that means the player plays hard all the time and is always in the action - defending, rebounding, diving for loose balls, and running the court. A coach can learn a lot about a player's work ethic by how he does the little things during a game. And when a player is clearly playing harder than anyone in the gym, coaches notice.

3. Character. Whether the is player coachable, dependable, unselfish, and a good teammate are important character traits to many college coaches. A college coach who is considering offering a scholarship to a player is inviting that player into his extended family for the next four years. He knows that player will be a reflection of him to the public and to the university who employs him. A player with poor character can derail a team quickly and be a distraction if he creates issues in the locker room or outside the locker room. Coaches can learn a lot about a player's character by watching how they play and interact with teammates, officials, and coaches.

A player's athletic ability and basketball skills are necessary to get him into consideration, but for many players it's the intangibles that differentiate him from the other players who have similar abilities. Whether it's a high school game or a travel game or just a training session, develop all three of these abilities. Get objective feedback, and remember, the coaches are not only watching what you can do but they are also interested in how you do it.

Assessing the "Offer"

An "offer" is what college programs do when they are recruiting a player and get to the point where they decide they want to "offer" a player a scholarship to attend their school. The problem with the "offer" is that it's not an official document or binding agreement that the school is making with the athlete. In many cases the "offer" is extended verbally over the phone or in a conversation on campus with an athlete and his or her family.

Because every school has a slightly different approach to scholarship offers and there is no way to really verify an "offer" was made other than asking the coach who allegedly made it, the whole "offer" process can be misleading for parents and players. We talk to parents all of the time who claim their player has been "offered" by schools we know have not "offered" them. Sometimes the parent just truly doesn't know the difference between an offer and interest. Other times the parent is exaggerating an interaction with college coaches in order to puff up their own egos or promote their kid. When you hear the father of a eighth grader start bragging about the number of offers received, there is a good chance they have "confused" what really constitutes an offer.

Here are some of those interactions that do not qualify as real "offers":

- If you receive a form letter or other marketing material from a college basketball program, that doesn't mean you have been offered.
- If you receive an invitation from a college coach to visit campus for an official or an unofficial visit, that doesn't mean you have been offered.
- If a college coach tells you that he likes your game a lot, that doesn't mean you have been offered.
- If a college coach tells you that he is going to recruit you, that doesn't mean you have been offered.
- If a college coach tells you that you are a priority recruit, that doesn't mean you have been offered.

- If a college coach attends your game or practice, that doesn't mean you have been offered.
- If a college coach texts you, emails you, or calls you regularly, that doesn't mean you have been offered.
- If a college coach tells you they hope you will walk on to the team, that doesn't mean you have been offered.

You will know you have been offered a scholarship by a school when a coach from the program (usually the head coach, but not always) says to you, "I want to offer you a scholarship to attend XYZ school." If you ever have any doubts, just ask the coach you are communicating with to clarify. For example, "Hi, Coach, I know you said you really liked my game and you wanted to recruit me. Does that mean you are offering me a scholarship now?" or "My travel coach said you had offered me a scholarship. I just wanted to make sure that was exactly what you said? Are you offering me a scholarship?"

The problem with an official offer is that there is nothing official about it. The process varies depending on the program. In some programs the head coach presents the offer. In other programs the assistant coach does. Sometimes the offer is first communicated to a player's high school coach or parent and then the player. In other cases the player gets the offer. Sometimes the offer is made in person and sometimes it's made over the phone.

What do you do if a college coach does officially offer you?

It's a big deal when a college coach says he wants to make a $100,000 investment in you. Start with gratitude. Whether you are really excited about the offer or not, thank the coach for being willing to make that kind of commitment to you.

You might also want to clarify the offer as well. If they don't say, you might ask if they are offering a full scholarship or a partial scholarship?

If you receive an offer you don't need to feel obligated to respond right away. You could say something like:

"Thanks for the offer, Coach. This is something I want to discuss with my parents. I would like to come visit your school sometime in the future as well."

You might want to ask the coach if they have a timeline for your decision on accepting the offer. They may ask you the same thing. Just answer honestly and let the coach know what you think your timeline might look like. For example, you might say, "I would like to visit some schools this fall and try to make a final decision at the beginning of my high school season."

As you go through the recruiting process, remember that a scholarship offer is not binding. A college coach does not have to honor an offer later. It's also not uncommon for a school to rescind an offer because of a player's behavior, grades, or actions of people associated with the player (parents, AAU coaches, friends, etc . . .). Just because a school has offered you today doesn't mean that offer is going to be good forever. Remember, the coach offering to invest $100,000 in you has his own career and family to think about as well. In many cases a school may be recruiting several players to fill one position knowing that some will not choose their school.

This doesn't mean you need to panic and "commit" to the first program who offers you. Just be responsible, communicate with the coaching staff, continue to work on your game, and do your homework. Once you have done your homework (i.e., made official visits, met with staff, discussed with your parents and high school coach) then you may want to give the program you want to choose the acknowledgement that you want to accept their offer. If you have done your homework and are confident in your choice, then go ahead and let the coach know of your decision.

We also recommend giving the other coaches who are recruiting you and have offered you the courtesy of personally letting them know you won't be choosing their school and express appreciativeness for their interest.

You Never Know Who is Watching

A couple of years ago I attended a local high school game, which highlights the importance of always playing as if a college coach is watching. At this particular game I arrived just after tip and sat toward the top of the bleachers. It was a Tuesday night game in January and there weren't many people in the stands; nobody really seemed to notice my presence either. I happened to have the HoopSeen Twitter account open on my phone and sent a tweet about being at this particular game.

One of the guards on the home team was in his junior year and was starting to gain more and more interest from a number of Division I schools. However, no college coaches were in attendance that night to watch. I had heard from the player's high school coach that he was putting up good numbers and I was interested to see him play. Statistically speaking he had a decent game and showed some really excellent flashes of playmaking and athleticism. But something seemed off with him personally. He pouted almost every time a play didn't go his way, he talked back to his coach, and appeared visibly frustrated almost the entire game. His negative body language was obvious and even distracting to anyone watching.

I didn't think too much of it, but on the way home from the game I got a call from our editor-in-chief of HoopSeen, Justin Young. Many college coaches follow our HoopSeen social media accounts and one of the schools recruiting the player I had just watched had seen the tweet from the beginning of the game (that "HoopSeen" was in attendance) and had called Justin as soon as the game had ended wondering if Justin had been there. Justin then called me to get my feedback to pass along to the program recruiting this particular player I had just watched.

What caught me off guard was the question about the player we will call Adam (not his real name).

Almost as if he had just seen the game himself Justin asked, "How was Adam's body language and attitude tonight?"

61

I answered honestly that it was not good. I explained how I had noticed it the entire game and shared how he talked back to the coach and was hard on his teammates and didn't seem like he even wanted to be there.

Then Justin relayed the conversation to me with that he had just had with one of the school's who was recruiting Adam. He said he had just got off the phone with XYZ University and that they may offer him but they have been worried about his attitude and body language and how he will fit with the culture of their program. They wanted feedback on how things went tonight. The feedback they were looking for had nothing to do with Adam's abilities. They were already more than convinced that he had the skills and athleticism to help them. They wanted feedback on his attitude, particularly during a game where Adam might think nobody "important" was watching.

I relay this story because as a player you never know when your opportunity might come or slip away. I am not sure if the presence of college coaches or knowledge that a person from an influential scouting service was in the building would have changed Adam's approach that night. He may have had the same bad attitude, but regardless of how Adam handled it, the moral of the story is that if you are playing high school ball you should assume every time you step on the court that you may have an opportunity to take one step closer or farther away from a college scholarship.

Whether an actual college coach is watching or a scouting service, every practice, training session and game should be treated like they are watching. Even if nobody is paying attention, you will develop the kind of habits that college coaches want. Moreover, the coach on the other team might regularly talk to college coaching buddies about the players his team faces in the region. A parent of one of your teammates might have played college basketball and have former coaches or teammates still in the game. You never know who can connect the dots that will shape your future.

I don't consider myself a scout. We have people on our staff at HoopSeen who are much better at evaluating players than myself. I was at this particular game as a fan. If I hadn't happened to tweet something on the HoopSeen Twitter account nobody would have known I was there otherwise. But chance happened and I was put in a position to give feedback to a college about what I saw from a player. They cared about he played but more importantly they cared about how he carried himself. How are you doing? Are you different when people are watching than when they aren't (or you think they aren't)? You never know when or how or through whom your next opportunity might come.

Questions Players Should Ask on a Recruiting Visit

General Student Athlete Questions
- What is the living situation like?
- What is the meal plan/athlete's nutrition plan?
- How many people will I live with?
- How close is housing to the gym/practice facility?
- Where do the players hang out?
- How do you travel to games?
- What do you like the most about XYZ University, Coach?

Academic Questions
- Who is the academic adviser?
- How do student athletes take tests/study/take classes during road games and travel conflicts?
- Do I have to take summer classes?
- What percentage of your players graduate in four years?
- What major do most players pursue? Are there any majors players are discouraged from pursuing?

Basketball Program Questions
- How many players have you offered at my position?
- How many players are already on the roster at my position?
- What percentage of freshmen recruited remains with the team all four years?
- What are the off-season requirements for your players?
- What are the redshirt procedures and do you plan on me redshirting my freshman year?

Do's and Don'ts of Recruiting

DO's
1. Meet with your high school coach or travel coach and get some honest feedback on what level of college basketball he thinks you can play.
2. Meet with a guidance counselor to ensure you are on the right track to qualify academically.

64

3. Once you have a good sense of the level of program you could potentially play for do some research and make a target list of potential schools.
4. Write letters to the schools on your target list expressing interest in learning more about the program.
5. Have a full game film put together. This is not a mixtape or highlight video.
6. Find a good service to host your recruiting video online and send the coaches at your target schools a link to the video.
7. Find a good travel program to play on during the spring and summer. Don't choose a program based on the name and its affiliations. Make sure it is a good fit for you and also a situation where you will have an opportunity to play in front of college coaches.
8. Attend "elite" summer camps of schools who genuinely show interest in you and where you might want to go play. A form letter or marketing email does not mean a school is interested.

Don'ts

1. Don't reject feedback from a credible coach about his opinion of what level you can play in college. Parents in particular are almost never objective about the true ability of their child and it can cost the athlete in the long run.
2. Don't bombard college coaches with emails, texts, and other communication constantly "hyping" your game. At the minimum you will annoy coaches, but you could even end up dissuading a school from recruiting you.
3. Don't lie or mislead about the true nature of how recruitment is going. College coaches and scouts talk and it will impact your reputation and credibility when the truth is known.
4. Don't choose a travel team because of the brand of their shoes. Find the best situation, coach, and system to highlight your skills and college coaches will find you.
5. Don't post stupid or offensive things on your social media accounts. If college coaches recruit you, they will follow you.
6. Don't pout, fight, loaf, or talk back to travel coaches and/or referees whether college coaches are in the building or not. You never know who is watching.
7. Don't forget to get your academics straight from the beginning of high school.

In their own words: Advice from college coaches about the recruiting process.

"Two questions we ask early on: Is he a good student? Is he a good person? If those cannot be answered favorably, it is going to be hard for us to recruit you regardless of your basketball talent."

"Colleges are watching EVERYTHING--how you are with teammates, who you interact with off court, what teachers think of you, etc . . ."

"Be respectful, listen to, and evaluate any college that is interested in you. Don't treat your interaction with coaches differently depending on your perception of the "level" of that school. Most recruits have a very unrealistic view of their "level" so don't drop calls from a school that when it's all said and done you would've landed at focusing on other names."

"Be coachable, be a team player, be a good person, and surround yourself with people who truly have your best interest at heart. Keep your circle small and tight."

"Worry less about rankings and recruiting and just focus on getting better and winning."

"Be yourself and have fun with the process and good things will happen. Never get too high or too low. If you're doing positive things both on and off the floor, coaches will find you."

"Maximize your potential with a great attitude, academics, hard work, coachability, winning and a winning attitude, consistent skill development, and athletic training. If you want to limit, hurt, or destroy your recruitment, show POOR attitude, academics, hard work, coachability, winning and a winning attitude. All of these categories will be evaluated in this highly competitive decision making process of building a WINNING TEAM and PROGRAM and having options as a potential student-athlete."

"Don't get caught up in the hype and don't take yourself so seriously. Just work hard and care most about the success of your team and your teammates in the process."

"As a coach I'm gonna watch you in a lot of different environments: practice, conditioning, and games. Have the same energy and toughness every time you're in a gym."

"Have info together. Short highlight clip, full game film, transcript, SAT/ACT scores, contact info, parents' employment, coach contact info. Register for NCAA Eligibility Center as a soph in HS no matter what."

"Define and write down your "fit." Too many people are throwing this word around without defining it. Reduce your list off an objective process. Second, tighten up your circle as opposed to expanding it during the process. Keep it within the family if possible. The more you let in, the more confusing it will get. Not as many people have your best interest at heart as you think!"

"Play on a summer team that you are going to PLAY on! No one wants to see you on the bench."

"Worry about winning and being a good teammate. Selfishness sticks out. Trying to "be seen" stands out in the worst way. Winning stands out in the best way. Good players are defined by those who do the most to help their team win. Good players are not defined by players who score a lot of points or have sports enter like highlights on bad teams."

"Keep your circle tight. Make sure the people around you have your best interests at heart. Also, think before you hit "post.""

"Don't become enamored with the recruiting process. Your ultimate goal shouldn't be getting a scholarship offer. Your goal should be to become a great college player. The number of offers you have doesn't dictate that."

"If you want to be a part of a great program, be a great MAN. Be a good person, be honest, be on time, be a friend, treat women with respect, treat coaches and adults with respect, etc."

"To enjoy the process and be in control of their recruitment. It is their life not their coaches, parents, etc. Make sure they are working towards their goals and to never be satisfied in life and basketball with lack of effort, enthusiasm, and anything other than a positive attitude."

"Don't try to do things that you can't because people tell you it's what coaches want to see from you."

"Work on your game and the recruitment will come. Spend more time on your game and less time on promoting your game."

"Be aware that you are always being evaluated...on the court and off. How you treat your teachers, coaches, teammates, and parents is very important."

APPENDIX I - NCAA Division I Schools by Conference

AMERICA EAST CONFERENCE
University at Albany, SUNY
Binghamton University
University of Hartford
University of Maine
University of Maryland, Baltimore County
University of New Hampshire
Stony Brook University
University of Vermont

AMERICAN ATHLETIC CONFERENCE
University of Central Florida
University of Cincinnati
University of Connecticut
East Carolina University
University of Houston
University of Memphis
University of South Florida
Southern Methodist University
Temple University
Tulane University
University of Tulsa

ATLANTIC 10
Davidson College
University of Dayton
Duquesne University
Fordham University
George Mason University
George Washington University
La Salle University
University of Massachusetts Amherst
University of Rhode Island

University of Richmond
St. Bonaventure University
Saint Joseph's University
Saint Louis University
Virginia Commonwealth University

ATLANTIC COAST CONFERENCE
Boston College
Clemson University
Duke University
Florida State University
Georgia Institute of Technology
University of Louisville
University of Miami
University of North Carolina at Chapel Hill
North Carolina State University
University of Notre Dame
University of Pittsburgh
Syracuse University
University of Virginia
Virginia Tech
Wake Forest University

ATLANTIC SUN CONFERENCE
Florida Gulf Coast University
Jacksonville University
Kennesaw State University
Lipscomb University
New Jersey Institute of Technology
University of North Florida
University of South Carolina Upstate

69

Stetson University

BIG 12 CONFERENCE
Baylor University
Iowa State University
University of Kansas
Kansas State University
University of Oklahoma
Oklahoma State University–
Stillwater
University of Texas at Austin
Texas Christian University
Texas Tech University
West Virginia University
BIG EAST CONFERENCE
Butler University
Creighton University
DePaul University
Georgetown University
Marquette University
Providence College
St. John's University
Seton Hall University
Villanova University
Xavier University

BIG SKY CONFERENCE
California State University,
Sacramento
Eastern Washington University
University of Idaho
Idaho State University
University of Montana
Montana State University
University of North Dakota
Northern Arizona University
University of Northern Colorado
Portland State University
Southern Utah University
Weber State University

BIG SOUTH CONFERENCE
Campbell University
Charleston Southern University
Gardner–Webb University
High Point University

Liberty University
Longwood University
University of North Carolina at
Asheville
Presbyterian College
Radford University
Winthrop University

BIG TEN CONFERENCE
University of Illinois at Urbana–
Champaign
Indiana University
University of Iowa
University of Maryland, College
Park
University of Michigan
Michigan State University
University of Minnesota
University of Nebraska–Lincoln
Northwestern University
The Ohio State University
Pennsylvania State University
Purdue University
Rutgers University
University of Wisconsin–Madison

BIG WEST CONFERENCE
University of California, Davis
University of California, Irvine
California Polytechnic State
University
University of California,
Riverside
University of California, Santa
Barbara
California State University,
Fullerton
California State University, Long
Beach
California State University,
Northridge
University of Hawaii at Manoa

COLONIAL ATHLETIC
ASSOCIATION
College of Charleston

University of Delaware
Drexel University
Elon University
Hofstra University
James Madison University
University of North Carolina at Wilmington
Northeastern University
Towson University
College of William & Mary

CONFERENCE USA
University of Alabama at Birmingham
Florida Atlantic University
Florida International University
Louisiana Tech University
Marshall University
Middle Tennessee State University
University of North Carolina at Charlotte
University of North Texas
Old Dominion University
Rice University
University of Southern Mississippi
University of Texas at El Paso
University of Texas at San Antonio
Western Kentucky University

HORIZON LEAGUE
Cleveland State University
University of Detroit Mercy
University of Illinois at Chicago
Northern Kentucky University
Oakland University
Valparaiso University
University of Wisconsin–Green Bay
University of Wisconsin–Milwaukee
Wright State University
Youngstown State University

IVY LEAGUE
Brown University
Columbia University
Cornell University
Dartmouth College
Harvard University
University of Pennsylvania
Princeton University
Yale University

METRO ATLANTIC ATHLETIC CONFERENCE
Canisius College
Fairfield University
Iona College
Manhattan College
Marist College
Monmouth University
Niagara University
Quinnipiac University
Rider University
Saint Peter's University
Siena College

MID-AMERICAN CONFERENCE
University of Akron
Ball State University
Bowling Green State University
University at Buffalo
Central Michigan University
Eastern Michigan University
Kent State University
Miami University
Northern Illinois University
Ohio University
University of Toledo
Western Michigan University

MID-EASTERN ATHLETIC CONFERENCE
Bethune-Cookman University
Coppin State University
Delaware State University
Florida A&M University
Hampton University

Howard University
University of Maryland Eastern
Shore
Morgan State University
Norfolk State University
North Carolina Agricultural and
Technical State University
North Carolina Central University
Savannah State University
South Carolina State University

MISSOURI VALLEY
CONFERENCE
Bradley University
Drake University
University of Evansville
Illinois State University
Indiana State University
Loyola University Chicago
Missouri State University
University of Northern Iowa
Southern Illinois University
Carbondale
Wichita State University

MOUNTAIN WEST
CONFERENCE
Boise State University
California State University,
Fresno
Colorado State University
University of Nevada, Las Vegas
University of Nevada, Reno
University of New Mexico
San Diego State University
San Jose State University
United States Air Force Academy
(Air Force)
Utah State University
University of Wyoming

NORTHEAST CONFERENCE
Bryant University
Central Connecticut State
University
Fairleigh Dickinson University

Long Island University–Brooklyn
Mount St. Mary's University
Robert Morris University
Sacred Heart University
St. Francis College
Saint Francis University
Wagner College

OHIO VALLEY CONFERENCE
Austin Peay State University
Belmont University
Eastern Illinois University
Eastern Kentucky University
Jacksonville State University
Morehead State University
Murray State University
Southeast Missouri State
University
Southern Illinois University
Edwardsville
University of Tennessee at Martin
Tennessee State University
Tennessee Technological
University

PAC-12 CONFERENCE
University of Arizona
Arizona State University
University of California, Berkeley
University of California, Los
Angeles
University of Colorado Boulder
University of Oregon
Oregon State University
University of Southern California
Stanford University
University of Utah
University of Washington
Washington State University

PATRIOT LEAGUE
American University
Boston University
Bucknell University
Colgate University
College of the Holy Cross

Lafayette College
Lehigh University
Loyola University Maryland
United States Military Academy
(Army)
United States Naval Academy
(Navy)

SOUTHEASTERN
CONFERENCE
University of Alabama
University of Arkansas
Auburn University
University of Florida
University of Georgia
University of Kentucky
Louisiana State University
University of Mississippi
Mississippi State University
University of Missouri
University of South Carolina
University of Tennessee
Texas A&M University
Vanderbilt University

SOUTHERN CONFERENCE
The Citadel
East Tennessee State University
Furman University
Mercer University
University of North Carolina at
Greensboro
Samford University
University of Tennessee at
Chattanooga
Virginia Military Institute
Western Carolina University
Wofford College

SOUTHLAND CONFERENCE
University of Central Arkansas
Houston Baptist University
Lamar University
McNeese State University
University of New Orleans
Nicholls State University

Northwestern State University
Sam Houston State University
Southeastern Louisiana
University
Stephen F. Austin State
University
Texas A&M University–Corpus
Christi

SOUTHWESTERN ATHLETIC
CONFERENCE
Alabama Agricultural and
Mechanical University
Alabama State University
Alcorn State University
University of Arkansas at Pine
Bluff
Grambling State University
Jackson State University
Mississippi Valley State
University
Prairie View A&M University
Southern University
Texas Southern University

SUN BELT CONFERENCE
Appalachian State University
University of Arkansas at Little
Rock
Arkansas State University
Coastal Carolina University
Georgia Southern University
Georgia State University
University of Louisiana at
Lafayette
University of Louisiana at
Monroe
University of South Alabama
University of Texas at Arlington
Texas State University
Troy University

THE SUMMIT LEAGUE
University of Denver
Indiana University – Purdue
University Fort Wayne

Indiana University – Purdue University Indianapolis
University of Nebraska Omaha
North Dakota State University
Oral Roberts University
University of South Dakota
South Dakota State University
Western Illinois University

WEST COAST CONFERENCE
Brigham Young University
Gonzaga University
Loyola Marymount University
University of the Pacific
Pepperdine University
University of Portland
Saint Mary's College of California

University of San Diego
University of San Francisco
Santa Clara University

WESTERN ATHLETIC CONFERENCE
California State University, Bakersfield
Chicago State University
University of Missouri–Kansas City
New Mexico State University
Seattle University
University of Texas Rio Grande Valley
Utah Valley University

APPENDIX II - NCAA Division II Schools by Conference

CALIFORNIA COLLEGIATE ATHLETIC ASSOCIATION
California State Polytechnic University, Pomona
California State University, Chico
California State University, Dominguez Hills
California State University, East Bay
California State University, Los Angeles
California State University, Monterey Bay
California State University, San Bernardino
California State University, Stanislaus
University of California, San Diego
Humboldt State University
San Francisco State University
Sonoma State University

CONFERENCE CAROLINAS
Barton College
Belmont Abbey College
Converse College
Erskine College
King University
Lees–McRae College
Limestone College
University of Mount Olive
North Greenville University
Pfeiffer University
Southern Wesleyan University

CENTRAL ATLANTIC COLLEGIATE CONFERENCE
Bloomfield College
Caldwell University
Chestnut Hill College
Concordia College
Dominican College
Felician University
Georgian Court University
Goldey–Beacom College
Holy Family University
Nyack College
Philadelphia University
Post University
University of the Sciences
Wilmington University

CENTRAL INTERCOLLEGIATE ATHLETIC ASSOCIATION
Bowie State University
Chowan University
Elizabeth City State University
Fayetteville State University
Johnson C. Smith University
Lincoln University (PA)
Livingstone College
Saint Augustine's University
Shaw University
Virginia State University
Virginia Union University
Winston–Salem State University

EAST COAST CONFERENCE
University of Bridgeport
Daemen College

University of the District of
Columbia
Long Island University–Post
Mercy College
Molloy College
New York Institute of
Technology
Queens College
Roberts Wesleyan College
St. Thomas Aquinas College

GREAT AMERICAN
CONFERENCE
Arkansas Tech University
University of Arkansas at
Monticello
East Central University
Harding University
Henderson State University
Northwestern Oklahoma State
University
Ouachita Baptist University
Southeastern Oklahoma State
University
Southern Arkansas University
Southern Nazarene University
Southwestern Oklahoma State
University

GREAT LAKES
INTERCOLLEGIATE
ATHLETIC CONFERENCE
Ashland University
Ferris State University
University of Findlay
Grand Valley State University
Hillsdale College
Lake Erie College
Lake Superior State University
Michigan Technological
University
Northern Michigan University
Northwood University
Ohio Dominican University
Saginaw Valley State University
Tiffin University

Walsh University
Wayne State University

GREAT LAKES VALLEY
CONFERENCE
Bellarmine University
Drury University
University of Illinois at
Springfield
University of Indianapolis
Lewis University
Maryville University
McKendree University
Missouri University of Science
and Technology
University of Missouri–St. Louis
Quincy University
Rockhurst University
Saint Joseph's College
University of Southern Indiana
Truman State University
William Jewell College
University of Wisconsin–Parkside

GREAT MIDWEST ATHLETIC
CONFERENCE
Alderson Broaddus University
Cedarville University
Davis & Elkins College
Kentucky Wesleyan College
Malone University
Ohio Valley University
Trevecca Nazarene University
Ursuline College

GREAT NORTHWEST
ATHLETIC CONFERENCE
University of Alaska Fairbanks
University of Alaska Anchorage
Central Washington University
Montana State University Billings
Northwest Nazarene University
Saint Martin's University
Seattle Pacific University
Simon Fraser University
Western Oregon University

Western Washington University

GULF SOUTH CONFERENCE
University of Alabama in Huntsville
Christian Brothers University
Delta State University
Lee University
Mississippi College
University of North Alabama
Shorter University
Union University
Valdosta State University
University of West Alabama
University of West Florida
University of West Georgia

HEARTLAND CONFERENCE
University of Arkansas – Fort Smith
Dallas Baptist University
Lubbock Christian University
Newman University
Oklahoma Christian University
Oklahoma Panhandle State University
Rogers State University
St. Edward's University
St. Mary's University
Texas A&M International University

INDEPENDENT
Bluefield State College
Oakland City University
Salem International University

LONE STAR CONFERENCE
Angelo State University
Cameron University
Eastern New Mexico University
Midwestern State University
Tarleton State University
Texas A&M University–Commerce

Texas A&M University–Kingsville
Texas Woman's University
University of Texas of the Permian Basin
West Texas A&M University
Western New Mexico University

MID-AMERICA INTERCOLLEGIATE ATHLETICS ASSOCIATION
University of Central Missouri
University of Central Oklahoma
Emporia State University
Fort Hays State University
Lincoln University (MO)
Lindenwood University
Missouri Southern State University
Missouri Western State University
University of Nebraska at Kearney
Northeastern State University
Northwest Missouri State University
Pittsburg State University
Southwest Baptist University
Washburn University

MOUNTAIN EAST CONFERENCE
University of Charleston
Concord University
Fairmont State University
Glenville State College
Notre Dame College
Shepherd University
Urbana University
University of Virginia's College at Wise
West Liberty University
West Virginia State University
West Virginia Wesleyan College
Wheeling Jesuit University

NORTHEAST-10
CONFERENCE
Adelphi University
American International College
Assumption College
Bentley University
Franklin Pierce University
Le Moyne College
Merrimack College
University of New Haven
Pace University
Saint Anselm College
Saint Michael's College
College of Saint Rose
Southern Connecticut State
University
Southern New Hampshire
University
Stonehill College

NORTHERN SUN
INTERCOLLEGIATE
CONFERENCE
Augustana University
Bemidji State University
Concordia University–St. Paul
University of Mary
Minnesota State University,
Mankato
Minnesota State University
Moorhead
University of Minnesota
Crookston
University of Minnesota Duluth
Minot State University
Northern State University
St. Cloud State University
University of Sioux Falls
Southwest Minnesota State
University
Upper Iowa University
Wayne State College
Winona State University

PACIFIC WEST CONFERENCE

Academy of Art University
Azusa Pacific University
Brigham Young University–
Hawai'i
California Baptist University
Chaminade University of
Honolulu
Dixie State University
Dominican University of
California
Fresno Pacific University
Hawai'i Pacific University
University of Hawai'i at Hilo
Holy Names University
Notre Dame de Namur University
Point Loma Nazarene University

PEACH BELT CONFERENCE
Armstrong State University
Augusta University
Clayton State University
Columbus State University
Flagler College
Francis Marion University
Georgia College & State
University
Georgia Southwestern State
University
Lander University
University of Montevallo
University of North Carolina at
Pembroke
University of North Georgia
University of South Carolina
Aiken
Young Harris College

PENNSYLVANIA STATE
ATHLETIC CONFERENCE
Bloomsburg University of
Pennsylvania
California University of
Pennsylvania
Cheyney University of
Pennsylvania

78

Clarion University of Pennsylvania
East Stroudsburg University of Pennsylvania
Edinboro University of Pennsylvania
Gannon University
Indiana University of Pennsylvania
Kutztown University of Pennsylvania
Lock Haven University of Pennsylvania
Mansfield University of Pennsylvania
Mercyhurst University
Millersville University of Pennsylvania
University of Pittsburgh at Johnstown
Seton Hill University
Shippensburg University of Pennsylvania
Slippery Rock University of Pennsylvania
West Chester University of Pennsylvania

ROCKY MOUNTAIN ATHLETIC CONFERENCE
Adams State University
Black Hills State University
Chadron State College
Colorado Christian University
Colorado Mesa University
Colorado School of Mines
Colorado State University–Pueblo
University of Colorado Colorado Springs
Fort Lewis College
Metropolitan State University of Denver
New Mexico Highlands University
Regis University

South Dakota School of Mines and Technology
Western State Colorado University

SOUTH ATLANTIC CONFERENCE
Anderson University
Brevard College
Carson–Newman University
Catawba College
Coker College
Lenoir–Rhyne University
Lincoln Memorial University
Mars Hill University
Newberry College
Queens University of Charlotte
Tusculum College
Wingate University

SOUTHERN INTERCOLLEGIATE ATHLETIC CONFERENCE
Albany State University
Benedict College
Central State University
Claflin University
Clark Atlanta University
Fort Valley State University
Kentucky State University
Lane College
LeMoyne–Owen College
Miles College
Morehouse College
Paine College
Tuskegee University

SUNSHINE STATE CONFERENCE
Barry University
Eckerd College
Florida Southern College
Florida Institute of Technology
Lynn University
Nova Southeastern University
Palm Beach Atlantic University
Rollins College

Saint Leo University
University of Tampa

APPENDIX III - NCAA Division III Schools by Conference

ALLEGHENY MOUNTAIN COLLEGIATE CONFERENCE
D'Youville College
Franciscan University of Steubenville
Hilbert College
La Roche College
Medaille College
Mount Aloysius College
Pennsylvania State University, Altoona
Pennsylvania State University, Erie
University of Pittsburgh at Bradford
University of Pittsburgh at Greensburg

AMERICAN SOUTHWEST CONFERENCE
Belhaven University
Concordia University Texas
East Texas Baptist University
Hardin–Simmons University
Howard Payne University
LeTourneau University
Louisiana College
University of Mary Hardin–Baylor
McMurry University
University of the Ozarks
Sul Ross State University
University of Texas at Dallas
University of Texas at Tyler

CAPITAL ATHLETIC CONFERENCE
Christopher Newport University
Frostburg State University
University of Mary Washington
Marymount University
Pennsylvania State University, Harrisburg
St. Mary's College of Maryland
Salisbury University
Southern Virginia University
Wesley College
York College of Pennsylvania

CENTENNIAL CONFERENCE
Bryn Mawr College
Dickinson College
Franklin & Marshall College
Gettysburg College
Haverford College
Johns Hopkins University
McDaniel College
Muhlenberg College
Swarthmore College
Ursinus College
Washington College

CITY UNIVERSITY OF NEW YORK ATHLETIC CONFERENCE
Baruch College
Brooklyn College
City College of New York (CCNY)
Hunter College
John Jay College of Criminal Justice
Lehman College
Medgar Evers College
College of Staten Island

York College, City University of New York

COLLEGE CONFERENCE OF ILLINOIS & WISCONSIN
Augustana College
Carroll University
Carthage College
Elmhurst College
Illinois Wesleyan University
Millikin University
North Central College
North Park University
Wheaton College

COLONIAL STATES ATHLETIC CONFERENCE
Cabrini University
Cairn University
Cedar Crest College
Centenary College of New Jersey
Gwynedd Mercy University
Immaculata University
Keystone College
Marywood University
Neumann University
Notre Dame of Maryland University
Rosemont College
Clarks Summit University

EMPIRE 8
Alfred University
Elmira College
Hartwick College
Houghton College
Ithaca College
Nazareth College
St. John Fisher College
Stevens Institute of Technology
Utica College

GREAT NORTHEAST ATHLETIC CONFERENCE
Albertus Magnus College
Anna Maria College

Emmanuel College
Johnson & Wales University
Lasell College
Mount Ida College
Norwich University
Rivier University
University of Saint Joseph
Saint Joseph's College of Maine
Simmons College
Suffolk University

HEARTLAND COLLEGIATE ATHLETIC CONFERENCE
Anderson University
Bluffton University
Defiance College
Earlham College
Franklin College
Hanover College
Manchester University
Mount St. Joseph University
Rose-Hulman Institute of Technology
Transylvania University

INDEPENDENT
Alfred State College
University of California, Santa Cruz
Finlandia University
Illinois Institute of Technology
University of Maine at Presque Isle
Maranatha Baptist University
Mills College
Mount Mary University
College of New Rochelle
State University of New York at Canton
Pine Manor College
Rust College
Trinity Washington University
University of Valley Forge
Berea College

IOWA INTERCOLLEGIATE
ATHLETIC CONFERENCE
Buena Vista University
Central College
Coe College
University of Dubuque
Loras College
Luther College
Nebraska Wesleyan University
Simpson College
Wartburg College

LANDMARK CONFERENCE
Catholic University of America
Drew University
Elizabethtown College
Goucher College
Juniata College
Moravian College
University of Scranton
Susquehanna University

LIBERTY LEAGUE
Bard College
Clarkson University
Hobart College
Rensselaer Polytechnic Institute
Rochester Institute of Technology
St. Lawrence University
Skidmore College
Union College
Vassar College
William Smith College

LITTLE EAST CONFERENCE
Eastern Connecticut State
University
Keene State College
University of Massachusetts
Boston
University of Massachusetts
Dartmouth
Plymouth State University
Rhode Island College
University of Southern Maine
Western Connecticut State
University

MAC COMMONWEALTH
CONFERENCE
Albright College
Alvernia University
Arcadia University
Hood College
Lebanon Valley College
Lycoming College
Messiah College
Stevenson University
Widener University

MAC FREEDOM
CONFERENCE
Delaware Valley University
DeSales University
Eastern University
Fairleigh Dickinson University,
Florham
King's College
Manhattanville College
Misericordia University
Wilkes University

MASSACHUSETTS STATE
COLLEGIATE ATHLETIC
CONFERENCE
Bridgewater State University
Fitchburg State University
Framingham State University
Massachusetts College of Liberal
Arts
Massachusetts Maritime
Academy
Salem State University
Westfield State University
Worcester State University

MICHIGAN
INTERCOLLEGIATE
ATHLETIC ASSOCIATION
Adrian College
Albion College
Alma College
Calvin College

Hope College
Kalamazoo College
Olivet College
Saint Mary's College
Trine University

MIDWEST CONFERENCE
Beloit College
Cornell College
Grinnell College
Illinois College
Knox College
Lake Forest College
Lawrence University
Monmouth College
Ripon College
St. Norbert College

MINNESOTA
INTERCOLLEGIATE
ATHLETIC CONFERENCE
Augsburg College
Bethel University
Carleton College
Concordia College
Gustavus Adolphus College
Hamline University
Macalester College
College of Saint Benedict
St. Catherine University
Saint John's University
Saint Mary's University of
Minnesota
St. Olaf College
University of St. Thomas

NEW ENGLAND
COLLEGIATE CONFERENCE
Bay Path University
Becker College
Daniel Webster College
Elms College
Lesley University
Mitchell College
Newbury College
Regis College

Southern Vermont College
Wheelock College

NEW ENGLAND SMALL
COLLEGE ATHLETIC
CONFERENCE
Amherst College
Bates College
Bowdoin College
Colby College
Connecticut College
Hamilton College
Middlebury College
Trinity College
Tufts University
Wesleyan University
Williams College

NEW ENGLAND WOMEN'S &
MEN'S ATHLETIC
CONFERENCE
Babson College
Clark University
Emerson College
Massachusetts Institute of
Technology
Mount Holyoke College
Smith College
Springfield College
United States Coast Guard
Academy (Coast Guard)
Wellesley College
Wheaton College
Worcester Polytechnic Institute

NEW JERSEY ATHLETIC
CONFERENCE
Kean University
Montclair State University
The College of New Jersey
New Jersey City University
Ramapo College
Rowan University
Rutgers University–Camden
Rutgers University–Newark
Stockton University

William Paterson University

NORTH ATLANTIC
CONFERENCE
Castleton University
Colby–Sawyer College
Green Mountain College
Husson University
Johnson State College
Lyndon State College
University of Maine at
Farmington
Maine Maritime Academy
New England College
Thomas College

NORTH COAST ATHLETIC
CONFERENCE
Allegheny College
Denison University
DePauw University
Hiram College
Kenyon College
Oberlin College
Ohio Wesleyan University
Wabash College
Wittenberg University
College of Wooster

NORTHEASTERN ATHLETIC
CONFERENCE
Bryn Athyn College
Cazenovia College
Gallaudet University
Keuka College
Lancaster Bible College
Morrisville State College
State University of New York at
Cobleskill
State University of New York
Polytechnic Institute
Pennsylvania College of
Technology[A 2]
Pennsylvania State University,
Abington

Pennsylvania State University,
Berks College
College of Saint Elizabeth
Wells College
Wilson College

NORTHERN ATHLETICS
COLLEGIATE CONFERENCE
Alverno College
Aurora University
Benedictine University
Concordia University Chicago
Concordia University Wisconsin
Dominican University
Edgewood College
Lakeland College
Marian University
Milwaukee School of Engineering
Rockford University
Wisconsin Lutheran College

NORTHWEST CONFERENCE
George Fox University
Lewis & Clark College
Linfield College
Pacific Lutheran University
Pacific University
University of Puget Sound
Whitman College
Whitworth University
Willamette University

OHIO ATHLETIC
CONFERENCE
Baldwin Wallace University
Capital University
Heidelberg University
John Carroll University
Marietta College
University of Mount Union
Muskingum University
Ohio Northern University
Otterbein University
Wilmington College

OLD DOMINION ATHLETIC
CONFERENCE
Bridgewater College
Eastern Mennonite University
Emory and Henry College
Guilford College
Hampden–Sydney College
Hollins University
Lynchburg College
Randolph College
Randolph–Macon College
Roanoke College
Shenandoah University
Sweet Briar College
Virginia Wesleyan College
Washington and Lee University

PRESIDENTS' ATHLETIC
CONFERENCE
Bethany College
Chatham University
Geneva College
Grove City College
Saint Vincent College
Thiel College
Thomas More College
Washington & Jefferson College
Waynesburg University
Westminster College

SKYLINE CONFERENCE
Farmingdale State College
Mount Saint Mary College
College of Mount Saint Vincent
State University of New York
Maritime College
State University of New York at
Old Westbury
State University of New York at
Purchase
Russell Sage College
St. Joseph's College (Brooklyn)
St. Joseph's College (Long Island)
Sarah Lawrence College
Yeshiva University

United States Merchant Marine
Academy (Merchant Marine)

SOUTHERN ATHLETIC
ASSOCIATION
Berry College
Birmingham–Southern College
Centre College
Hendrix College
Millsaps College
Oglethorpe University
Rhodes College
Sewanee: The University of the
South
SOUTHERN CALIFORNIA
INTERCOLLEGIATE
ATHLETIC CONFERENCE
California Institute of Technology
California Lutheran University
Chapman University
Claremont–Mudd–Scripps
University of La Verne
Occidental College
Pomona College and Pitzer
College
University of Redlands
Whittier College

SOUTHERN COLLEGIATE
ATHLETIC CONFERENCE
Austin College
Centenary College of Louisiana
Colorado College
University of Dallas
Schreiner University
Southwestern University
Texas Lutheran University
Trinity University

ST. LOUIS
INTERCOLLEGIATE
ATHLETIC CONFERENCE
Blackburn College
Eureka College
Fontbonne University
Greenville College

Iowa Wesleyan College
MacMurray College
Principia College
Spalding University
Webster University
Westminster College

STATE UNIVERSITY OF NEW
YORK ATHLETIC
CONFERENCE
Buffalo State College
State University of New York at
Brockport
State University of New York at
Cortland
State University of New York at
Fredonia
State University of New York at
Geneseo
State University of New York at
New Paltz
State University of New York at
Oneonta
State University of New York at
Oswego
State University of New York at
Plattsburgh
State University of New York at
Potsdam

THE COMMONWEALTH
COAST CONFERENCE
Curry College
Eastern Nazarene College
Endicott College
Gordon College
University of New England
Nichols College
Roger Williams University
Salve Regina University
Wentworth Institute of
Technology
Western New England University

UNIVERSITY ATHLETIC
ASSOCIATION

Brandeis University
Carnegie Mellon University
Case Western Reserve University
University of Chicago
Emory University
New York University (NYU)
University of Rochester
Washington University in St.
Louis

UPPER MIDWEST ATHLETIC
CONFERENCE
Bethany Lutheran College
Crown College
Martin Luther College
University of Minnesota Morris
North Central University
Northland College
University of Northwestern – St.
Paul
The College of St. Scholastica
University of Wisconsin–Superior

USA SOUTH ATHLETIC
CONFERENCE
Agnes Scott College
Averett University
Covenant College
Ferrum College
Greensboro College
Huntingdon College
LaGrange College
Mary Baldwin College
Maryville College
Meredith College
Methodist University
North Carolina Wesleyan College
Piedmont College
Salem College
Wesleyan College
William Peace University

WISCONSIN
INTERCOLLEGIATE
ATHLETIC CONFERENCE

University of Wisconsin–Eau Claire

University of Wisconsin–La Crosse

University of Wisconsin–Oshkosh

University of Wisconsin–Platteville

ewater

University of Wisconsin–River Falls

University of Wisconsin–Stevens Point

University of Wisconsin–Stout

University of Wisconsin–Whit

Made in the USA
Columbia, SC
12 June 2018